HISTORICAL Gurdwaras of Delhi

ਨਰਾਇਣੁ ਕਲਾਧਾਰਿ ਜਗ ਮਹਿ ਪਰਵਰਿਯਉ ॥

HISTORICAL
Gurdwaras of Delhi

M.K. Pal

Foreword: Dr. Jaspal Singh

NIYOGI
BOOKS

Published by

NIYOGI BOOKS

D-78, Okhla Industrial Area, Phase-I
New Delhi-110 020, INDIA
Tel: 91-11-26816301, 49327000
Fax: 91-11-26810483, 26813830
email: niyogibooks@gmail.com
website: www.niyogibooks.com

Photographers: Shri Anoop Asthana, Sardar Amreek Singh Panesar, M.K. Pal, Shri Anil Bhatia
Editor: Supriya Mukherjee/Niyogi Books
Design: Shashi Bhushan Prasad/Niyogi Books

ISBN: 978-93-81523-48-3

Publication: 2013

Printed at: Niyogi Offset Pvt. Ltd., New Delhi, India

This book is dedicated to Sardar Khushwant Singh,
a prolific author who has written many books on the Sikh faith.

ਸ੍ਰੀ ਹਰਿਕ੍ਰਿਸ਼ਨ ਧਿਆਈਐ ਜਿਸੁ ਡਿਠੈ ਸਭਿ ਦੁਖਿ ਜਾਇ

God created Himself, and assumed a Name,
Second besides Himself, He created Nature,
Seated in Nature He watches
With delight what He creates.

—Guru Nanak: Asa-di-Var 1:3

There are the lowest among the low castes.
Nanak, I shall go with them. What have I got to do with the great?
God's eyes of mercy fall on those who take care of the lowly.

—Guru Nanak: Sri Rag

I do not go to Haj, to Ka'ba,
Nor do I go to any Tirtha for worship,
I worship only one god, and nobody else.

—Guru Arjan Dev

The man who receives the Grace of the Guru,
Discovers this secret of spiritual life;
Sayeth Nanak: The soul of such a man blends with
Almighty as water mixes with water.

—Hymn sung by Guru Tegh Bahadur: Rag Sorath

The same God dwells in the temple and the mosque,
The Hindus worship Him and the Muslims pray to Him.
Human beings are all one though of diverse forms,
Gods, demons, Yakshas and the minstrels divine.
The Muslims and Hindus are all one,
Imbibe they the influence of environs they inhabit.
Similar eyes, ears, body they have,
They are made of earth, air, fire and water alike,
Allah and Abekh are the names of the same one,
Whom adore the holy Puranas and Quran,
All are of the same form,
And one in their making.

—Guru Gobind Singh: Akal Ustat

ੴ

Mool Mantar

ੴ
ਸਤਿਨਾਮੁਕਰਤਾਪੁਰਖੁਨਿਰ
ਭਉਨਿਰਵੈਰੁਅਕਾਲਮੂਰ
ਤਿਅਜੂਨੀਸੈਭੰਗੁਰਪ੍ਰਸਾ
ਦਿ ॥ਜਪੁ॥ ॥ ॥

Ek Onkar Sat Naam Karta Purakh Nirbhau-Nirvair
Akal Murat Ajuni Saibhan Gur Parsad

Mool Mantar is the basic doctrine of Guru Nanak's philosophy of religion, and is laid in the very beginning of *Japji.* The basic *mantra* can be split in two aspects. The first aspect is *Ek Onkar* which declares its absolute value that 'God is one and the only Supreme Lord of all the existence'. The second aspect depicts the seven values of the Ultimate Reality as serialized in the *Mool Mantar*. These are: *Sat Naam* (Eternal Truth), *Karta Purakh* (the Creator and an Absolute Whole), *Nirbhau-Nirvair* (Who fears none and is nobody's Enemy), *Akal Murat* (An Immortal with personality beyond time), *Ajuni* (Neither dies nor is reborn), *Saibhan* (Who is self created), and *Gur Parsad* (He can only be realised if and when the *Guru* grants it).

(Reference: Narinder Singh Kohli, *Dhur Ki Bani: Nitnem)*

Contents

Foreword

Dr. M.K. Pal is a noted scholar, having previously dealt with several projects related to art and culture. His present book, entitled *Historical Gurdwaras of Delhi* is an honest and descriptive itinerary of visits to the historical Gurdwaras of Delhi.

The dominant idea permeating his work is the focus on how the historical Gurdwaras revive and revitalize the perennial spirit of Sikhism in the minds and psyche of the Sikhs!

Dr. Pal has interwoven his document with befitting anecdotes and legends associated with these centres of worship. The grandeur and splendour of these majestic centres of Sikh pilgrimages has been depicted by him in a succinct and coherent manner. A significant aspect of his writing is the emphasis on how the Gurus pronounced the ideal of a new social order, free from ritualistic boundaries embracing one and all!

Guru Nanak, the founder of the Sikh faith, followed his mission of vehemently denouncing and disparaging the prevailing social evils of all kind, especially those associated with various religions and denominations of the time, in a most compassionate and judicious manner. His mission was carried forward by the succeeding Gurus, who laid the foundation of various institutions and enunciated a code of ethics to be adhered to by the Sikhs. I hope, all these aspects which are nicely covered in this well-researched work, should have a deep impact on the minds of the reader.

Dr. Jaspal Singh
Vice-Chancellor
Punjabi University
Patiala

Introduction

The book titled *Historical Gurdwaras of Delhi* is intended to provide historical and socio-cultural information considered necessary to rightly understand the importance of the historical shrines of Delhi for the followers of a great religion—Sikhism. Sikhism as a religion has made significant contribution in promoting the concepts of peace, love, unity, national integration and universal brotherhood. The book is also intended to provide necessary information on the subject to the English-speaking/English-reading non-Punjabi public, and prospective pilgrims and visitors to these Gurdwaras. These Gurdwaras, many of which according to Sikh chronicles are consecrated by the Gurus' visits, are located in different parts of the city. A list of the historical Gurdwaras of Delhi in order of their period of construction is mentioned below:

1. *Gurdwara Nanak Piau Sahib*
2. *Gurdwara Majnu Tilla Sahib*
3. *Gurdwara Bangla Sahib*
4. *Gurdwara Bala Sahib*
5. *Gurdwara Sis Ganj Sahib*
6. *Gurdwara Rakab Ganj Sahib*
7. *Gurdwara Moti Bagh Sahib*
8. *Gurdwara Damdama Sahib*

Facing page: *The Khanda, the insignia of the Khalsa, is one of the most important symbols of Sikhism.*

Pages 10-11: *A view of Gurdwara Bangla Sahib alongwith the Sarovar (bathing tank) constructed on the model of the Sarovar of the Harimandir (Golden Temple) in Amritsar.*

9. *Gurdwara Mata Sundari*
10. *Gurdwara Baba Banda Singh Bahadur*

It deserves mention here that the Gurdwaras listed at serial numbers 1-8 are not only historical Gurdwaras but also known as historical shrines sanctified by the Gurus' visits, while the last two Gurdwaras listed at serial numbers 9 and 10 are historical Gurdwaras and not historical shrines as these two Gurdwaras were not consecrated by any Guru's visit.

Before we go for an in-depth study of the historical Gurdwaras of Delhi, it is perhaps pertinent to get an understanding of the circumstances under which the religion itself was born, and how Guru Nanak gave: "Practical effect to the doctrine that the lowest is equal to the highest, in race as in creed, in political rights as in religious hopes"(1).

State of affairs in the fifteenth century

Guru Nanak, the founder of Sikhism was born in 1469 C.E., in the second half of the fifteenth century C.E. It was an era of great social and religious ferment in the country and of great political instability.

Guru Nanak, First Guru of the Sikhs and Founder of Sikhism (1469-1539 C.E.).

Before Guru Nanak, some religious reformers and saints namely, Vallabhacharya, Chaitanya Mahaprabhu, Kabir, Namdev and Mira Bai, had done commendable works to rid religion of ritualism and had enriched literature in many ways, but most of them considered life as futile and did not give much thought to building up a new social order. It was Guru Nanak who perceived the true principles of social reform, and laid the foundations of a broad-based religion based on the spirit of equality among all sections of people. Guru Nanak's new religion was not only for the good of a particular community but also for the good of undivided humanity.

In fifteenth century India, there was a great decline in the religious sphere. Over-emphasis on ritualism and ceremonialism had become the bane of Hinduism, and had led to corruption, hypocrisy and delusion. It had also led to concentration of power in the hands of the priests who had grown selfish and covetous, and did not at all hesitate to exploit the illiterate and credulous masses. The Hindu society was divided into four castes namely, the *Brahmin*s, the *Kshatriya*s, the *Vaishya*s and the *Sudra*s.The only section of the society which stood to gain was the class of *Brahmin*s. The *Sudra*s did not enjoy any respect in society. The caste system had degenerated itself and instances are not wanting when the people belonging to the lowest class helped the Muslim invaders against their rulers.

In fifteenth century Punjab, the Muslims too suffered from caste hierarchy. They were divided into Shias and Sunnies. Externalism and ceremonialism were rampant among them, and the Mullahs and the Kazis grew fat at the expense of the common believer in Prophet Mohammad. Though the Muslims did not suffer so much from the evils of caste rigidity as did the Hindus, their religion needed as much reform.

In the social sphere, the Hindus were divided into various castes and sub-castes and it was difficult for them to present a united front to the foreign invaders (specially the Arabs, the Turks and the Pathans on their way to Delhi via Punjab). The Muslim rulers imposed *Jazia*, a pilgrimage tax on all non-Muslims, and subjected them to great indignities. On the other hand, the Muslim *Fakir*s were extended favours and privileges that were denied to the Hindu *Sadhu*s. There was thus complete social segregation between the non-Muslims and the Muslims, and the masses were greatly demoralized. The time was now ripe for the emergence of a great leader who could infuse a spirit of equality and freedom among the non-Muslims.

In the political sphere, the conditions were no better. The empire of the Lodis was fast dwindling and Babur was busy laying the foundations of the Mughal empire in the country. Enraged by the opposition offered to him by some Hindu *Zamindar*s, Babur ordered a general massacre of the people and made a large number of women slaves. According to one source, "Guru Nanak who happened to be present in the town, was also subjected to cruel treatment and made to carry heavy loads of looted property"(2).

Though these facts portray a rather dark side of the fifteenth century, it is important to remember that events of great significance took place during the same century not only in India but also elsewhere in the world. There was a spiritual renaissance in India spearheaded by saints like Ravidas and Kabir (1440-1518 C.E.) in Uttar Pradesh, Namdeva and Eknath (1528-1603 C.E.) in Maharashtra and Narsi Mehta in Gujarat. Among the contemporaries of Guru Nanak, the following deserve a special mention: Vallabhacharya (1479-1503 C.E.) who had a large number of followers in Gujarat and Rajasthan; Chaitanya Mahaprabhu (1486-1533 C.E.) who flourished in Orissa and roused the people of the province to great religious fervour; Mirabai (1499-1570 C.E.)—born in a royal household in Rajputana, and the great poet Saint Tulsidas (1533-1624 C.E.) who was born in Uttar Pradesh and wrought a great spiritual revolution in the lives of the people by his immortal Ramcharita Manas.

Though these saint poets had influence in their local areas, none of them travelled to other lands to spread their philosophy. The first saint to have travelled more than 40,000 kilometres and spread his message to the people of several countries, was Guru Nanak (Dr. Harjinder Singh Dilgeer: Sikh Twarikh).

Events of great significance also took place in Europe in the fifteenth century. There was a great intellectual and spiritual revolution. The discoveries and inventions such as the discovery of America by Columbus in 1492 C.E., Vasco-da-Gama's voyage by sea route to India in 1497 C.E., the theory of Copernicus (famous Astronomer: 1473-1543 C.E.) that the earth moves around the sun, and the invention of the printing press in 1450 C.E. brought about the great movement known as the Renaissance. At a later date, Martin Luther (1483-1546 C.E.), raised the banner of revolt against the degenerate Roman Catholicism and started the great reform movement within Christianity which is known as the famous religious revolution of the sixteenth century C.E. Historians believe that there is some sort of a parallel drawn between the reforms sought to be introduced by Guru Nanak in South Asia and those proposed by Luther in Christianity.

In the beginning of the sixteenth century C.E., when Guru Nanak was in the prime of his youth, Punjab was part and parcel of the vast empire of Delhi which was ruled by the Lodis (1451 C.E.-1526 C.E.). The scenario was one of chaos and confusion. There were uninterrupted scenes of tyranny and bloodshed. The country was utterly weak and disunited. The rulers had lost all sense of justice and fair play. The political, cultural and religious situations were disturbing. Guru Nanak, who was alive to the exigencies of the times, bitterly criticized the rulers. He said:

The Kal age is a drawn sword,
Kings are butchers,
Justice has taken wings and fled.
In this dark night of falsity,
the moon of truth is not visible.
I am bewildered and in this darkness no path is visible (3).

The masses were ignorant, backward and steeped in superstitions. They believed in prejudices. "The spirit of both Hinduism and Islam was hidden beneath a mass of formalities and extraneous observances. Tyranny reigned supreme, the tyranny of might, the tyranny of forms and the tyranny of names"(4).

The Muhammedan king was considered as *"Zil-e-Ilahi"* meaning "Shadow of God on earth". The Muslim subjects were the favourite children of the state. They alone were entitled to occupy high offices. Besides, they were given many other concessions. The non-Muslims, on the other hand, were considered infidels. They had to pay additional taxes like *Jazia* (the pilgrimage tax). Though the Muslims in general enjoyed some privileges, it was only the upper class amongst them who led a luxurious life at the cost of the poor and the lowly. The Muslims regarded the non-Muslims as their slaves and treated them with great disdain.

The people as a whole lost their moorings. They were poor, illiterate and fed on superstitions. The inhuman treatment they received at the hands of the rulers deprived them of self-respect. Religion had lost its sanctity and moral standards were completely forsaken. Political lawlessness, social confusion, and spiritual slavery were the order of the day. The rich tradition of religious tolerance was powerless against the tyranny and extreme bigotism of the epoch. Dissent was carried to a point of intolerance. The warriors had desires to conquer and achieve worldly gains. The invaders had trampled on the rich civilization of the country without the slightest remorse. "There is no one who receiveth or giveth not bribes. The king administers justice only when his palm has been greased (filled)"(5).

From tenth century onwards, successive hordes of invaders had poured in from Central Asia. As the highway to Delhi lay through Punjab, the greatest suffering had been caused to the people of this province. Guru Nanak was sent to earth by the almighty under such circumstances to bring peace and to present to mankind the image only of undivided humanity. In his passion to fulfil the divine mission entrusted to him, Guru Nanak travelled far and wide. It was Guru Nanak who laid the foundation of universal brotherhood, tolerance, amity and mutual affection. He emphasized the virtues of hard work, honest living, simple and quiet life, sympathy for the needy and the poor, and contentment. He condemned greed, avarice and high-handedness.

Guru Nanak's travels and his visit to Delhi

During his travel, Guru Nanak's message was to seek the core of each faith, and he led men to the path of goodness and virtue, and kindled the flame of love and goodwill in the hearts of millions of countrymen.

Guru Nanak, having attained enlightenment started his journey to redeem the world with God's name, when he was in his twenties. "I left my home in search of the righteous and followed this course to evolve a new philosophy of life. Being a pedlar of truth, I am out to trade in truth. It is through the righteous that I shall ferry my followings across the ocean of existence" (6).

He sought God's service through the service of mankind, becoming the Lord's bard. His travels are called *Udasi*s and said to be four in number:

- First *Udasi* 1507 C.E.-1515 C.E.
- Second *Udasi* 1516 C.E.-1517 C.E.
- Third *Udasi* 1518 C.E.-1521 C.E.
- Fourth *Udasi* 1521 C.E.-1522 C.E.

It appears that Guru Nanak completed his *Udasi*s during the period of about 15 years from 1507 C.E. to 1522 C.E. It deserves special mention in this context that Guru Nanak's *Udasi*s were undertaken in an epoch-making period. "The period of adventure, discovery, inquiry and renaissance. The adventures and discoveries not only led to physical achievements, but also to colonization, domination, oppression and invasion, while the inquiry and renaissance led to the search into human existence and reformation in the oppressive systems"(7). Thus, the purpose of Guru Nanak's *Udasi*s was also to draw the attention of erring humanity from the unreal, and from external ceremonies to inner purification.

Guru Nanak's First *Udasi* was eastward. According to *Janamsakhi Sodhi Meharban* (biography especially one of the early biographical-cum-hagiographical accounts of Guru Nanak by the author Sodhi Meharban), the Guru proceeded to the east and reached Delhi wherefrom he went to Hardwar. According to *Puratan Janamsakhi Walait Wali* (old biographical-cum-hagiographical accounts of Guru Nanak, Walait Wali) before turning east, the Guru went to Tulamba (Modern Makhdumpur, West Pakistan) where he met one Sajjan, a thug who had built a temple and a mosque along the highway to attract Hindu and Muslim travellers who needed a night's lodging. During the night, Sajjan used to kill them and rob their belongings. Guru Nanak had sensed his ill intentions and during his stay in Sajjan's inn, asked his companion Mardana to sing a hymn which touched Sajjan's heart. He fell at the Guru's feet, confessed his past sins and became his follower. It was after this that the Guru went on to Panipat and Delhi. "But majority of the scholars accept the view that the Guru, when he left Sultanpur (District Kapurthala, Punjab) straightaway marched eastward and the Guru's visits to Eminabad (old town near Gujranwala Tulamba, Pakistan) came off much later. After Panipat the Guru visited Delhi and stayed at a place called, *Majnu-ka-Tilla*. This Majnu was a pious Fakir and wielded considerable influence" (8). There are, however, some scholars who believe that the Guru first arrived on the outskirts of Delhi near a well located now on the G.T. Karnal Road near Azad Pur (Gudmandi), and camped there for a period of three months and three days. During his stay in this camp, he met the *Sufi Fakir*, Majnu at his hermitage on the banks of the river Yamuna. This place is now known as Majnu Tilla (near Chandraval village).

Guru Nanak's visit to Delhi marks the beginning of the Great Guru's missionary activities in the capital of the ruling Lodis. Since Guru Nanak's visit to Delhi, "this Metropolitan city has been connected with Sikh history not only because it was the highest seat of political power during the first 300 years of the life of the Sikh community, but also because five of the ten Sikh Gurus actually visited the city, which witnessed two of them ending their earthly lives here" (9).

Guru Harkrishan, the eighth Guru was only eight years old when he died of an attack of smallpox. Guru Teg Bahadur, the ninth Guru, fell

Renovation/reconstruction work in progress in the Bangla Sahib Gurdwara complex.

victim to Mughal Emperor Aurangzeb's religious bigotry. "He became a martyr at the altar of dharma. He laid down his life for the protection of the Hindu dharma. He had fought for the people's right of freedom of worship. He saved the Hindu religion from total annihilation and the country as a whole from being converted into Dar-ul-Islam" (10). The Guru was beheaded here publically on November 11, 1675 C.E.

Guru Nanak had advised his followers to form themselves into *Sangat*s and build *Dharamsal*s where they could not only congregate for prayers but also for deliberation over matters of common religious and social concern. The *Dharamsal*s (literally religious places) which later came to be called Gurdwaras (Guru's door or threshold), were mostly recorded by the authors of *Janamsakhi*s, *Gurbilase*s and other chronicles. Though systematic research and documentation of historical Sikh Shrines was undertaken in the later part of the nineteenth century by some travellers and scholars like Pundit Tara Singh Narottam, Giani Gian Singh and Giani Thakur Singh, their studies were basically concerned with the historical aspects of each shrine. The proposed study of the historical Gurdwaras of Delhi is, however, aimed at focusing on not only the historical aspects, but also the socio-cultural aspects of these shrines, which may have had a huge bearing on the tenets of Sikhism.

The Gurdwara is the place of worship for the Sikhs. It is the hub of Sikh life, religious, ethical, social and cultural. Several social functions, which ought to be performed in the presence of *Guru Granth Sahib*, are often held in the Gurdwaras. Hence, the Gurdwara is used as a meeting centre where matters of common concern are discussed and decided upon. Some of the rites and ceremonies usually performed in the Gurdwaras are birth ceremony, naming ceremony, marriage ceremony and death ceremony.

However, the essential and central role of a Gurdwara is to function as a place of worship, especially congregational worship. For this reason, most of the Gurdwaras have buildings commodious enough for the needs of their respective *Sangat*s as well as for special functions such as religious festivals (*Gurpurb*s).

So far as the architecture of the Gurdwaras is concerned, *Karsevawale Sant*s, a band of dedicated builder followers of Sant Gurmukh Singh engaged in reconstructing/renovating and development of Gurdwara buildings and complexes through free voluntary labour and donations, have introduced and popularized a more or less standard design which may fairly be labelled as Sikh architecture. It is based on the model of the *Darbar Sahib* in Amritsar, although not exactly its copy. According to the model, newly built or rebuilt central buildings of Gurdwaras are square high-ceilinged halls with usually a gallery running along its walls at mid-height and a square *Prakash Asthan* in the centre. Every Gurdwara must have the *Nishan Sahib*, the Sikh flag, which is triangular in shape and saffron in colour except in the case of *Nihang*s who sport a dark blue flag. *Nishan Sahib* is the most essential distinguishing feature

Prakash Asthan of the Golden Temple, Amritsar.

of a Gurdwara. It is becoming common to have a *Sarovar* (bathing tank) near a Gurdwara.

Most of the historical Gurdwaras of Delhi do not possess the original structural values or artistic merits as they have been damaged, destroyed or reconstructed/renovated over the years. Especially in the year 1783 C.E. Sardar Baghel Singh of Karorsinghian *Misl* established seven Gurdwaras in Delhi. Since then there have been continuous changes and renovations in the architectural designs of the historical Gurdwaras in Delhi, and as a result the present structures of the Gurdwara buildings seldom exhibit any characteristics of old architectural heritage.

The data collected on the ten historical Gurdwaras of Delhi through field investigations and from other published secondary sources, throw light on various hitherto unknown aspects of historical as well as age-old socio-cultural heritage of the Sikh community of Delhi.

Nanak Piau Sahib

ੴ
ਸਤਿਨਾਮੁ ਵਾਹਿਗੁਰੂ
ੴ
ਸਤਿਨਾਮੁ ਕਰਤਾ ਪੁਰਖੁ ਨਿਰਭਉ ਨਿਰਵੈਰੁ
ਅਕਾਲ ਮੂਰਤਿ ਅਜੂਨੀ ਸੈਭੰ ਗੁਰਪ੍ਰਸਾਦਿ ॥

Historical background and associated myths and legends

Gurdwara Nanak Piau Sahib located on the old G.T. Karnal Road near Azadpur (*Gudmandi*) and in proximity of Shakti Nagar/Rana Pratap Bagh Town, is considered one of the most sacred places in Delhi, where Guru Nanak first arrived near a well during his first *Udasi*. The well was in a garden on the outskirts of Delhi. Guru Nanak is said to have camped here for several days and during his stay he used to draw water from the well and serve it to the travellers and others in need, while also propagating the tenets of Sikhism. On hearing the news of Guru Nanak's arrival, people started coming to this place in large numbers. To serve fresh and cold water to the thirsty passers-by with his own hands, the Guru not only got a deep well dug here, but also set up a permanent *Piau* at this place, which came to be called *Nanak Piau*. The garden in which the Guru rested soon became a shrine as well as a place of pilgrimage for thousands of people. The owner of the garden donated the shrine to the public, and called it Guru Nanak's shrine. Travellers rested here for the night in winters and during the day in summers. They were served food and cold water from the sacred well. Guru Nanak made it a missionary centre. It continued to function even after the Guru resumed his travels further to the East, under the charge of one of his disciples. In sacred memory of Guru Nanak's visit to this place, a Gurdwara was built here later on, and was named as Gurdwara Nanak Piau Sahib. Gyani Thakur Singh in his *Gurdwara Darshan* says,

Facing Page: *The old well (Piau) of Guru Nanak's time is still preserved.*

Pages 26-27: *Gurdwara Nanak Piau Sahib located on the old G.T. Karnal Road near Azadpur.*

"The original name of the shrine was Pau Sahib. Here Guru Nanak humbled a very haughty Sannyasin in a religious discourse" (11).

When Guru Nanak visited Delhi, Sikander Lodi was the Emperor of Delhi. He was a ruler who let loose a reign of oppression on the Hindus. Considering the social and political condition of the country then, Guru Nanak chose to dress in a way that would attract the attention of people from different creeds and communities. "He put a regular garb of a missionary which consisted of a mango-coloured jacket over which he flung a white sheet" (12). Guru Nanak's creed of love and service to the humanity is perhaps better echoed in the following words of Albert Schweitzer: "Whatever you have received more than others in health, in talents, in ability, in success, in a pleasant childhood, in harmonious conditions of home life, all this you must not take as a matter of course. In gratitude for your fortune, you must render in return some sacrifice of your own life for other lives. In the Holy *Guru Granth*, the Saint has given the highest exposition of secularism. He was really an incarnation of humanity. He specially emphasized on moral values, particularly on sympathy, piety and justice" (13).

While camping in the garden on the outskirts of Delhi, one day Guru Nanak saw the owners of an elephant crying bitterly over the body of the animal which they thought was dead (which was, in fact, not dead). The Guru asked them why they were weeping when their elephant was actually not dead. On hearing this, the extremely happy owners bowed their heads before the Guru and left for their home. In the course of time, news reached the Emperor (Sikander Lodi) that a non-Muslim *Fakir*, admired by both the Muslim and the Hindu divines of Delhi, had brought a dead elephant back to life. A few days later, the Emperor's elephant died, and he sent a message for Guru Nanak asking him to bring the dead animal back to life. The Guru smiled and said to the messenger that life and death are in the hands of the Almighty. Nobody can interfere with His mysterious ways. The answer silenced the messenger and his companions and they went home. Whatever may be the truth behind these stories, it can be assumed that Guru Nanak was against the performance of any miracle (*Karamat*), that may interfere in the ways of God.

Architectural details: An overview

The present Gurdwara building marks the site where Guru Nanak first arrived near a well (*Piau*). This is a new building constructed by Late Baba Harbans Singh Karsevawale (who left for his heavenly abode in April 2011) after demolishing the older one constructed by Dharam Singh and Vivek Singh (local residents) in 1960-62, in memory of their deceased parents. On the basis of a photograph of the building published in a book in 1976, it may be pointed out that the earlier building of the

Gurdwara Nanak Piau Sahib with a pinnacled dome has a spacious walled compound, entry into which is through a gateway on the G.T. Karnal Road.

Prakash Asthan of the Gurdwara Nanak Piau Sahib.

Gurdwara was in the form of a single storey Bungalow (*Bangla*) with a boundary wall and a wide entrance. According to Late Sardar Daryodh Singh, who used to be the oldest resident of the area, the building of the earlier Gurdwara was constructed on a solid foundation by Dharam Singh and Vivek Singh. At the time of its demolition in 1982, Late Sardar Daryodh Singh had earnestly requested Late Baba Harbans Singh not to demolish this building. Rather, he suggested, that a new building of the Gurdwara could be constructed alongside the older one keeping in view the sentiments expressed by the local residents. However, his requests fell on deaf ears. The construction of the new building of the Gurdwara Nanak Piau Sahib is reported to have started in 1982 and completed in 1992. It deserves mention in this context that in 1783 C.E. Sardar Baghel Singh was allowed by the then Mughal Emperor Shah Alam II to build seven historical Gurdwaras in Delhi. As there is no mention of Gurdwara Nanak Piau in the list of seven historical Gurdwaras built by Sardar Baghel Singh, it may be assumed that there was no need to build a Gurdwara at the site of Gurdwara Nanak Piau as there already existed a Gurdwara at the time of Sardar Baghel Singh's stay in Delhi for a period of one year.

Late Baba Harbans Singh Karsevawale who left for his heavenly abode in April 2011.

The newly constructed Gurdwara Nanak Piau Sahib is housed in a high-ceilinged flat-roofed square hall with an all-round mid-height gallery and a pinnacled dome. The *Guru Granth Sahib* (the Holy scripture of the Sikhs) is seated on a canopied seat of white marble in the middle of the hall. The Gurdwara complex has a spacious walled compound, entry into which is through a gateway on the G.T. Karnal Road. The *Sarovar* (sacred bathing tank) behind the Gurdwara makes for an additional attraction for the devotees and the visitors. The most important historical evidence still preserved in the Gurdwara complex is the old well (*Piau*) from Guru Nanak's times. The water of the well is not only considered sacred, but also believed to be containing medicinal properties. It is strongly believed here that when devotees offer heartfelt prayers near the well their prayers are answered.

The present Gurdwara is located in an area which was originally a part of an agricultural land. As reported by Late Sardar Daryodh Singh, the area was known as village Rajpura, old *Chhauni.* When he came to the village in 1949, the whole area was demarcated as cultivable land owned by the villagers. With time, the government started acquiring the land for setting up residential colonies. From 1960 onwards, a number of residential colonies have come up in the area, the most important of them being D.T.C. Colony, Sardar Nagar, New Gupta Colony, C.C. Colony, Kalyan Vihar, Kripal Ashram, Eshar Colony, Polo Ground (Near Police Line), and Gurmandi Bank Colony. Late Sardar Daryodh Singh purchased some acres of agricultural land from the villagers, but when the acquisition of such land for residential purpose was initiated by the government, Late Sardar Daryodh Singh's agricultural land was also notified for acquisition. However, he was permitted to retain a few acres of land which he had developed for setting up a residential colony for the Sikhs now known as Sardar Nagar, just a few yards from the Gurdwara Nanak Piau complex. Late Sardar Daryodh Singh had been living in the area for more than 50 years; at the fag end of his life he completely dedicated himself to offering prayers at his household shrine where the *Guru Granth Sahib* was seated, and paying a visit to the Nanak Piau Sahib every day. He was able to clearly recapitulate the history of the area and the activities pertaining to reconstruction and development of the building of Gurdwara Nanak Piau at 87 years of age. He was not an educated person, but his thoughtful comments on the reconstruction and development of Gurdwara buildings reflect his genuine concern about the preservation of our splendid Sikh heritage. A similar view expressed by Patwant Singh (a noted Sikh scholar) is mentioned below:

"While it is good to build new Gurdwaras, the destruction of the old is ill-advised. The new is another link in the continuation of history

Guru-ka-Langar where selfless service is offered for preparing food for all.

and the two have to co-exist with each other. One cannot replace it. As people around the world become increasingly conscious of the need to conserve their heritage, and are perfecting new techniques and skills for the preservation and restoration of history's artifacts, it will be tragic if we continue to neglect the relics of our rich past" (14).

Special programmes and socio-cultural activities

Gurdwara Nanak Piau Sahib is noted for arranging special programmes which include the celebration of Guru Nanak's birth anniversary on the full moon day of Kartik (November) and Guru Nanak Jyoti Jot Samavan. Special *Kirtan Darbar*s and special *Guru-ka-Langar*s are also arranged on various occasions.

The most important part of the service offered by Gurdwara Nanak Piau Sahib consists of corporate singing of *Kirtan* (devotional songs) and distribution of *Guru-ka-Langar* to the congregation at the end of the Sikh service. The community kitchen in the medieval *Sufi Khanqa*s was known as the *Langar*. It was open mostly to the inmates of the *Khanqa*s. The Sikh Gurus established a similar institution.

It is an established fact that the tradition of *Guru-ka-Langar* was started by Guru Nanak at Kartarpur (on the right bank of river *Ravi*: now in Pakistan) in 1522 C.E. and he built the first Sikh shrine and a community dining hall there. Later, it was made a compulsory feature of the Sikh service (which consists of corporate singing of devotional songs and distribution of *Guru-ka-Langar* to all human beings) by Guru Angad in 1539 C.E. He took special steps to popularise the institution of *Guru-ka-Langar*, the community kitchen. The main characteristics of the *Guru-ka-Langar* prescribed by the Sikh Gurus were: simplicity, that the food was simple and clean; equality, that the

The food prepared in the Guru-ka-Langar is open to all irrespective of caste, creed and nationality.

meals were served to all from the same bowl and that all present were seated together; service, that the food was prepared by the devotees themselves; vegetarian, that the food was vegetarian and was edible by all; *Bhog*, that the food was formally placed in front of the Guru (now the *Guru Granth Sahib*) before the *Ardas*, for God's blessings. *Guru-ka-Langar* is open to people of all nationalities and of all countries. The rich and the poor, and Hindus, Muslims and Christians, all sit in a row and eat the food to their heart's content.

The institution of *Guru-ka-Langar* is always associated with the institutions of *Sangat* (mixed congregations) and *Pangat* (row, line for serving *Guru-ka-Langar*). In order to give concrete expression to his ideas of unity, equality, and fraternity, Guru Nanak started the twin institutions of *Sangat* and *Pangat* by virtue of which high or low, rich or poor, men or women could sit together, pray together and dine together. The concept of *Sangat* was a dynamic contribution to the healthy growth and progress of man and society. "It aimed at improving the spiritual perception, ethical discipline and social harmony of the congregation. It had a distinct practical purpose of carrying the society forward towards collective enlightenment"(15). *Sangat* or *Sat-Sangat* as an institution is considered to possess, besides its social effect, high soteriological merit as well as epistemological value for acquiring higher knowledge. Theologically, *Sangat* is meant for practicing *Nam* and *Kirtan*. Guru Arjan Dev declared, "Singing of God's glory in holy congregation is the noblest of actions"(16). It is also said by the Sikh Gurus that an *Ardas* made by the *Sangat* was always accepted by God. They further said that God resided in *Sangat* and that *Sangat* was at par with the divine. In the *Guru Granth Sahib*, the creative role of the *Sangat* is repeatedly emphasized. Guru Nanak's institutions of *Sangat* and *Pangat*, therefore, brought before the people the vision of a classless democratic society, where all could claim equal status.

Gurdwara Nanak Piau Sahib also plays an important role in the socio-cultural life of the people of the nearby localities. On Sundays, the Gurdwara is visited by maximum number of devotees/visitors. Many of the visitors gather in the Gurdwara hall for spiritual solace and enlightenment, while some others come and join the worship in a congregation (*Sangat*). There prevails in the Gurdwara an atmosphere of complete peace and tranquility. The *Guru-ka-Langar* of the Gurdwara remains busy throughout the day. The community kitchen, therefore, appears to have played a significant role in forging the bond of love and a strong sense of unity among the people of the area, through the spirit of *seva* (selfless service).

Gurdwara Nanak Piau Sahib offers various educational facilities within the Gurdwara complex—it has the Co-educational Technical Institute and a public school named Guru Harkrishan Public School. The Gurdwara complex also has a hospital which provides free medical treatment to all. The Gurdwara makes special arrangements to accommodate people who visit from different places of North India, to take Unani medicine from a heart specialist residing in the C.C. Colony nearby.

All the activities undertaken by Gurdwara Nanak Piau Sahib bear testimony to the Sikh community's basic concept of the service of mankind. *Seva* means service or help, and true service removes ego and burns greed and hypocracy. As an individual, a Sikh must love others, help the needy, pay a tenth part of his earnings for noble causes and render physical service in the upkeep of the Gurdwara and the *Guru-ka-Langar*. The service of the sick, disabled, blind, poor, hungry and the old is the fundamental duty of a Sikh. However, a service performed without heart and spirit is deemed meaningless.

Karseva (same as *Seva*) has special significance in the Sikh religion. It refers to the voluntary service performed to maintain the Gurdwaras. From the days of Guru Nanak, till today, the Sikh Gurdwaras have been serviced with the labour of the devotees and also funded by the devotees at large and, "Not by monopolistic or oligopolistic donations of a few" (18).

Other relevant information

Gurdwara Nanak Piau Sahib has a special place in the history of the old Sikh Gurdwaras in Delhi because at this place a *Dharamsal* (place of worship) is said to have come into existence during the time of Guru Nanak, the founder of the Sikh religion. This was the first *Dharamsal* in Delhi which Guru Nanak used as a missionary centre. The second *Dharamsal* seems to have come into existence at Majnu Tilla, a place the Guru visited during his stay in Delhi and where he held long spiritual discourses with many *Yogi*s, *Sufi*s and *Fakir*s. Thereafter, Majnu Tilla became a missionary centre of Sikh faith. In the course of time, both the *Dharamsal*s were transformed into Gurdwaras.

Gurdwara Nanak Piau Sahib is visited by a large number of people everyday. Every year, the death anniversary of Guru Nanak is celebrated at the Gurdwara complex. Thousands of devotees gather here and pay their homage in the memory of the founder of the Sikh faith.

Majnu Tilla Sahib

ਗੁਰੂ ਹਰਿ ਗੋਬਿੰਦ
ਨਿਵਾਸ

Historical background and associated myths and legends

Gurdwara Majnu Tilla Sahib is one of the oldest historical Gurdwaras of Delhi. During his stay in Delhi, Guru Nanak also stayed at Majnu Tilla, where a Muslim ascetic (locally known as Majnu, a *Sufi Fakir* from Iraq) lived in a hermitage on the banks of the Yamuna river. He led a lonely life of penitence. When Guru Nanak blessed him, he achieved supreme enlightenment and became a devout disciple of the Guru. Guru Nanak held long discourses with him, which, changed Majnu's attitude towards faith from that of renunciation to a more balanced view. Majnu's hermitage thereafter became an outstanding missionary centre of Sikh faith for centuries to follow. To commemorate the holy visit of the Great Guru to his hermitage and to immortalize his own name, Majnu expressed a desire that his hermitage be named after him. The Guru granted his request and this place came to be known as *Majnu-ka-Tilla* (hillock of Majnu). Many *Sufi*s, *Yogi*s, *Vairagi*s and *Sant*s of Delhi came to Guru Nanak here and held spiritual discourses with him. "Conspicuous among those, who came to pay homage and were deeply influenced by Guru Nanak, was the *Sajjadanashin* (Caretaker of a Mausoleum) of the famous Mausoleum of Nizamuddin Aulia. He had mutual, heart-to-heart talk with Guru Nanak about divine love here at this sacred place" (19).

When Guru Hargobind (Sixth Guru of Sikhism), was invited by Emperor Jehangir, he came and stayed at Majnu Tilla. The suspicious

Facing page: *Gurdwara Majnu Tilla Sahib located on the banks of the river Yamuna near Chandraval village, close to I.S.B.T., Delhi.*

Pages 40-41: *When Guru Hargobind, the Sixth Guru of the Sikhs, was invited by the Emperor Jehangir, he came to Delhi and stayed at Majnu Tilla.*

Emperor arrested him at this very place, and imprisoned him at the Gwalior Fort. According to available historical evidence, Guru Hargobind succeeded Guru Arjan in 1606 C.E. during one of the most difficult times in the history of the Sikhs. Guru Arjan left the following injunction for his son and successor Guru Hargobind, before leaving his mortal coil: "I have succeeded in affecting the object of my life. Go to my son, the holy Hargobind, and give him from me ample consolation. Bid him not to mourn or indulge in unmanly lamentations, but sing God's praises. Let him sit fully armed on his throne, and maintain an army to the best of his ability. Let him affix the patch of Guruship to his forehead according to ancient custom, and ever treat his Sikhs with the utmost courtesy. Let him hold Bhai Buddha in honour, and in all respect, except the wearing of arms enjoined, adopt the practices of the preceding Gurus. Cremate not my body, but let it flow on the bossom of this river"(20).

Guru Hargobind, the Sixth Guru of the Sikhs (1595-1644 C.E.).

Before his death Guru Arjan was much harassed and put through many hardships by the Mughal Emperor Jehangir. Jehangir ascended the throne of the Mughal Empire at Agra after the death of Akbar, the Great. While Akbar had not interfered with the Sikh movement, the growing influence of the Gurus and the speed with which the Sikh movement was gaining momentum, perturbed Jehangir. He was trying to find some excuse to harm Guru Arjan. Chandu Lal, the Dewan of Lahore helped the Emperor in this conspiracy. Chandu told the Emperor that the Guru had helped the Emperor's son, Khusru, who had rebelled against him. The Emperor found an opportunity to give expression to his anger against the Guru and got him arrested under the charges of sedition. The Guru was brought to Lahore and under the orders of the Emperor, was handed over to Chandu who tortured him in the most gruesome ways. He was made to sit on red-hot iron and hot sand was poured over his naked body.

Nonetheless, the Guru remained calm and tranquil throughout these ordeals and went about reciting the holy hymns. At last, the Guru was forced to take a bath in the river Ravi. Chandu thought the Guru's body which was full of blisters, would experience greater agony when dipped in cold water. While taking a dip in the torrential river, the Guru drowned and his body could not be traced anywhere.

Before his martyrdom on May 30, 1606 C.E., Guru Arjan realised that it would no longer be "possible to preserve the Sikh community without the aid of arms"(21). Because of this realization he gave the injunction to Guru Hargobind that, the Sikhs could resort to arms for self-defence and preserving their honour. The supreme sacrifice made by Guru Arjan is a milestone in the history of the Sikhs. His martyrdom caused widespread resentment. The Sikhs looked upon this sacrifice from a totally different angle. As stated by Trumpp Earnest: 'His death is the great turning point in the development of the Sikh community as from that time this struggle commenced that changed the entire character of the reformatory religious movement"(22). Thus, after the death of Guru Arjan, the entire character of the Sikh movement changed radically. The Sikhs now had to resort to arms for self-defence.

Guru Arjan's son Guru Hargobind, tried his best to give shape to his father's last desire that he should have a nucleus of an army. "The young Guru issued a proclamation to Masands, that he would be pleased with those who could bring him offerings of arms and horses of good breed"(23). He made arrangements for imparting training to the Sikhs in the art of fighting. The Guru strengthened the city of Amritsar by constructing a fort, called Lohgarh. The Guru's efforts in militarising the Sikhs made Chandu Lal, the Dewan of Lahore, jealous and he became apprehensive of Guru Hargobind's rising popularity and power. Moreover, Chandu Lal's hostility against the Guru sprang from his father Guru Arjan's rejection of his daughter's hand for his son Guru Hargobind.He started to see the Guru as a potential source of threat to him, and as a result he started sending complaints to Emperor Jehangir to the effect that the Guru sat on a throne, kept arms and called himself the true king. The Emperor was also told that the Guru had taken a vow to avenge his father's death. Although Chandu Lal took his opportunity to add to the Guru's suffering, it is hardly likely that he had the influence to cause it. The real cause was the attitude of the Emperor himself. He felt especially alarmed at the growing influence of Guru Arjan, and he decided to summon the Guru to Delhi and admonish him.

The Emperor sent his representatives to summon the Guru. At first the Guru was reluctant to go to Delhi, but later decided to see the Emperor when his disciples said that it would provide him with an opportunity to apprise the Emperor of Chandu Lal's true character and to get his misdeeds investigated. The Guru started for Delhi in late 1612 C.E. On reaching Delhi he camped at Majnu Tilla. When Guru Hargobind appeared in the Emperor's *Darbar*, the Emperor without listening to the Guru, issued orders to confine him in the Gwalior fort prison for 12 years.

The Guru remained in prison for sometime. According to *Mohsin Fani*, "The Guru remained in prison for 12 years. However, some other scholars are of the opinion that the period of imprisonment was between two and five years" (24). According to latest research by Sikh scholars, the Guru remained in Gwalior fort prison from January 1613 to October 25, 1619 (Dr. H.S. Dilgeer: Sikh Twarikh). *Mohsin Fani* also tells us that during the period of the Guru's confinement, many faithful Sikhs used to come and bow before the walls of the Gwalior fort, "which restrained their persecuted Guru, till at last the Emperor moved, perhaps, as much by superstition as by pity, released him from confinement"(25). When he was released, he insisted that all other prisoners should also be released. The Guru, along with his own release, also brought about the release of his fifty-two fellow prisoners, mostly Rajas who had been confined in the Gwalior Fort. After his release from the prison and on his way back to Punjab, Guru Hargobind passed through Delhi and again stayed at Majnu Tilla for a day.

After the release of the Guru, cordial and friendly relations were established between the Guru and Emperor Jehangir who even surrendered Chandu Lal, the enemy of the Sikhs, into their hands. The wicked man was put to death by the angry Sikhs. So great was the cordiality between the Emperor and the Guru that they would usually go together on hunting expeditions.

When Aurangzeb occupied the throne of the Mughal Empire on July 21, 1658 C.E., the policy of peace received a setback. During his struggle for throne, Aurangzeb had to fight against his brother Dara Shikoh's army. Dara Sikoh lost the battle at Shamugarh and fled towards Punjab. On his way, he met Guru Har Rai (Guru Hargobind's grandson). At this, the enemies of Guru Har Rai got an opportunity to carry tales against the Guru to Aurangzeb. They poured venomous words into his ears and ultimately succeeded in turning him against the Guru. Aurangzeb was advised to call the Guru to Delhi, and, either punish him or convert him to Islam. As a result, Aurangzeb summoned Guru Har Rai to visit Delhi, but the Guru declined. Instead, Guru Har Rai asked his son Ram Rai to go to Delhi. Special instructions were given to Ram Rai by the Guru regarding what should be his conduct in the Emperor's court. The Guru strictly warned him against explaining any portion of the *Guru Granth Sahib* in any way different from what it actually meant. He was especially asked not to perform any miracles and interfere in the ways of God.

Ram Rai reached Delhi and stayed at Chandraval Khera (now Majnu Tilla). From here, he went to the court of the Mughal Emperor and he was received with due respect and honour. However, he forgot the instructions given by the Guru, and at the behest of Aurangzeb, Ram Rai performed several miracles (*Karamat*). This included one at Majnu Tilla, where, a well was dug and a sheet of cloth (*Chadar*) was spread over it. Ram Rai was asked to sit there. He sat on the *Chadar* confidently and no harm came to him. The *Chadar* did not budge an inch from its original place, even under the heavy weight of his body. Aurangzeb and the courtiers were all astonished to witness this miracle displayed by Ram Rai. It was believed that Ram Rai had supernatural powers, but his performance of miracles in the presence of the Emperor and the courtiers was against the basic principles of Sikhism.

During discussions in the Mughal court, Aurangzeb also discussed the Sikh philosophy with Ram Rai and asked him many probing questions. He wanted to know whether there was anything un-Islamic in the *Guru Granth Sahib*. Meanwhile, a courtier who was a mischief-monger and was able to read the holy scripture, pointed out a verse of Guru Nanak in the *Guru Granth Sahib*:

The ashes of the Muslim fall into the potter's clod;
Pots and bricks are made out of it.
And in the fire burns the poor clay.

—Asa-di-Var.

When Aurangzeb asked Ram Rai to explain the implication of these lines, he trembled and quailed in fright. Fearing Auranzeb's reaction to his explaining the verse in its true perspective, Ram Rai explained this portion of *Guru Granth Sahib* in a way different from what it actually meant. He said that the original words *Mitti Musalman ki* meaning the ashes of a Muslim, were a misprint and the correct words should be *Mitti Beiman ki* meaning the ashes of a cheat. Aurangzeb was satisfied with this response but Ram Rai made a folly of misrepresenting the truth of the verse in the *Guru Granth Sahib*. Actually, these lines expound the theory of Guru Nanak, that the soul of human beings leave the body and do not remain in the grave till doomsday.

Ram Rai's mistake of not following the instructions given by his father, Guru Har Rai, on the eve of his departure from Punjab, proved suicidal for him. When Ram Rai's perfidy was reported to the Guru, he was much annoyed and thought it to be an insult to Guru Nanak and his faith. He expressed his annoyance saying, "Let Ram Rai not look on my face again. Let him abide with Aurangzeb and amass money at his court". A month later, Guru Har Rai appointed his second son, Harkrishan, as his successor, eighth on the throne of Guru Nanak. He succeeded to the *gaddi* on October 6, 1661 C.E.

Considering the chain of events that took place, it may be assumed that even after Guru Nanak's death in 1539 C.E., the shrine of Majnu Tilla kept gaining in importance for over a century. The present Gurdwara Majnu Tilla Sahib is situated at a place, where an atmosphere of complete peace and tranquility prevails. As this historical shrine is somewhat away from the din and bussle of city life, it has become an ideal place for the devotees to seek the Lord's blessings through his remembrance.

Architectural details: An overview

As per the available historical evidence, Sardar Baghel Singh built a Gurdwara at Majnu Tilla in 1783 C.E. It was one of the seven historical Gurdwaras built by him with the permission of the then Mughal Emperor Shah Alam II.

The present building of the Gurdwara Majnu Tilla Sahib is a reconstructed one, and stands on a raised plinth with a doomed pavilion in the centre, and domed kiosks on the corners above the rooftop. The older building of the Gurdwara as seen in the photograph published in a book in 1976 (*The Sikh Gurus and their Shrines* by Surinder Singh Johar), was a simple single story building with a globular dome above the rooftop. The decorative pillars on the ground floor as shown in the photograph indicated that this building was perhaps designed with the idea of representing a *Bangla* (Bangalow). The present building of the Gurdwara, however, is a product of the last quarter of the twentieth century. It was rebuilt recently by Late Baba Harbans Singh (*Karsevawale*), who had been engaged in reconstructing and developing the Gurdwara buildings and complexes in Delhi.

The Gurdwara Majnu Tilla Sahib complex has another building just behind the main building of the Gurdwara. The construction of the building (as recorded in the memorial stone slab), was started in the year

1923 by Sardarni Harnam Kaur in memory of her late husband Sardar Ram Singh Kabli. The construction of the building was completed in 1950 and appears to have taken place in phases over a period of about 27 years. However, during the recent construction of the main Gurdwara building by Late Baba Harbans Singh, this building was not demolished. This building has a high-ceilinged hall with a square *Prakash Asthan* (sanctum sanctorum) in the middle of a side of the hall with a wooden dome. This building is mainly used for social ceremonies, *Path* and other customary practices. The main building of the Gurdwara Majnu Tilla Sahib facing north has a high-ceilinged big hall with 12 doors including the main entrance. The building has a square *Prakash Asthan* where the *Guru Granth Sahib* is seated, and has a gallery running along the inner walls of the building at mid-height. The deep well, which is said to have been dug up as a death trap for Guru Har Rai's son Ram Rai under the instruction of Aurangzeb is still preserved, and can be seen at the right-hand corner just opposite to the main entrace of the Gurdwara building.

The visitors and devotees coming from Punjab and other neighbouring states have a special attraction for Gurdwara Majnu Tilla Sahib. They prefer to stay at this Gurdwara before they visit other places in the capital. A new guest house has been constructed in the far end of the southern side of the Gurdwara complex by Late Baba Harbans Singh as extra accommodation for the incoming visitors.

Special programmes and socio-cultural activities

Among the daily programmes performed in this Gurdwara, the following call for a special mention:

- *Granth Sahib Da Prakash* (open state of *Guru Granth Sahib*).
- Recitation of five *Bani*s and *Sukhmani Sahib.*
- Recitation of *Nitnem*.
- Recitation of *Asa-di-Var*.

- Utterance of hymns from the *Guru Granth Sahib (Gurbani).*
- *Kirtan* (singing of scriptural hymns, devotional music specially *Sodar*).
- Recitation of *Rehra*s, containing nine hymns from the *Guru Granth Sahib.*
- *Arti kirtan* and *Sohila.*
- *Arda*s (supplicatory prayer); *Hukam*, and *Prasad* also form a part of the daily religious curriculum of the Gurdwara.

Kirtan, *Sohila*, *Ardas*, *Rehra*s, *Hukam* and *Karah Prasad* are all important parts of the daily religious rituals of any Gurdwara.

Kirtan: *Kirtan* consists of singing hymns (*Sabads* or *Shabad*s) from the *Guru Granth Sahib*. This is the main part of the Gurdwara service and it has been of paramount importance to the practice of Sikhism since the days of Guru Nanak. Nanak himself used to sing accompanied by his musician companion, Mardana, who played a stringed instrument. Generally in a Gurdwara, the musicians sit at the side of the canopy of the *Prakash Asthan* and this part of the service lasts for a few hours. *Kirtan* means far more to the Sikhs than simply the singing of hymns in God's praise, for it has a very strong mystical element, being the Word and Essence of God in the world, and the means to develop the spirituality of both the individual and the *Sangat*. According to R.S. Wahiwala, "Kirtan enters the body through the ears. It reaches the innermost cells and illuminates the unconscious self. The devotees, too, start singing along with the singers, thus they enter a state of trance, ecstacy and inner bliss. Kirtan is the food for thought, heart and soul"(26).

The significance of *Kirtan* can be gauged from the fact that the entire *Guru Granth Sahib* is set to music and is structured on the basis of Indian classical *raga*s in which the portions are supposed to be sung. "Guru Arjan, the compiler of the *Guru Granth Sahib*, arranged the sacred hymns on the basis of ragas and not on the basis of authorship or chronology"(27).

Sohila: This prayer is also a collection of hymns of the different Gurus. It contains three *Shabad*s of Guru Nanak, one *Shabad* of Guru Ram Das, and one *Shabad* of Guru Arjan. The hymns underline the pangs of separation of human beings from God, and the bliss they experience on being united with God again.

Ardas: *Ardas* means a humble request, supplication; it is a supplicatory prayer of the Sikhs. It is recited by the officiant leading the prayer alongwith the *Sangat. Ardas* is offered standing solemnly with folded hands. The whole congregation, including the *Granthi* faces the *Guru Granth Sahib* (placed at the *Prakash Asthan*) for offering *Ardas. Ardas* is best translated as, "To ask for what you desire" (Samsher Singh, *The Concept of Prayer in Sikhism*, SCI, Vol.28, no.66, 1988, p.6). It recalls the history of the Sikhs in the early years of Sikhism. *Ardas* is chanted by the *Granthi*, the congregation joining with responses of "*Waheguru*" (Wonderful Lord). *Ardas*, ends with the words "*Waheguru ji ka Khalsa*", to which the congregation responds with "*Waheguru ji ki fateh*". These two phrases put together mean, "The *Khalsa* is of God; the Victory is to God". Following this an untranslatable war cry is called in a loud triumphant voice, "*Jo bole so nihal!*", to which the congregation shouts, "*Sat Sri Akal*" (Truth is eternal). At the end of the *Anand* (greatest spiritual bliss), the *Guru Granth Sahib* is wrapped carefully in two white kerchiefs and is carried on the head to its place of rest, in a nearby special room, while the congregation sings; "*Sat Nam, Sat Nam, Sat Namji, Waheguru, Waheguru, Waheguruji*"(a chant at the end of the prayer).

Ardas means a humble request; it is a supplicatory prayer of the Sikhs. Ardas is offered standing solemnly with folded hands.

"When the *Guru Granth Sahib* is laid down, the call 'jo bole so nihal' is repeated and the congregation utters 'Sat Sri Akal', and touch their foreheads to the floor, and *Ardas* is over" (28).

Rehras: *Rehras* is a collection of hymns of five different Gurus. It contains five *Shabads* of Guru Nanak, two *Shabads* of Guru Ramdas, seven *Shabads* of Guru Arjan, six stanzas of *Anand Sahib* of Guru Amardas, one *Swayya*, *Dohira* and *Baentee Chaupai* of Guru Gobind Singh. *Rehras* as recorded in the *Guru Granth Sahib* contains hymns of only four Gurus and nine *Shabads* only, and the rest of the compositions were included in *Rehras* in the late nineteenth century C.E. The theme of the hymns is the description of the house of God and the mode to enter it.

Hukam: The word *Hukam* in the *Guru Granth Sahib* may be termed as "law", the divine law established by the sovereign God, under which the whole system of the created universe works. All other laws such as the metaphysical law of *Karma* and metempsychosis and laws of physics or biology are subsumed under *Hukam*. "All coming and going is by *Hukam*, everywhere, in front and behind, *Hukam* prevails". *(Guru Granth Sahib, 151)*. "Everything is within *Hukam*, none is outside *Hukam*'s pale; for one who understands *Hukam*, O Nanak, ego is non-existent" *(Guru Granth Sahib, 2)*. "Only those are made to accept *Hukam* on whom He bestows His Grace" *(Guru Granth Sahib, 510, 1027, 1423)*. "Those who are made to accept *Hukam* are complete men of the world; they serve their Master with full understanding of the *Shabad*". *(Guru Granth Sahib, 512)*.

"*Hukam* is the rule which determines the effect, action and fruit"(29). *Hukam* has been translated as, "God's Will, the eternal immutable and Universal laws of nature, divine decrees" (30). It has also been translated as "Will of God" and "The Writ of God". "*Hukam* as Universal Will or Divine Will can be understood to operate in two ways. It may be taken to operate as external to self as 'Thou shalt do this' as laid down in a series of commandments in scriptures" (31). But in another and proper sense, in Sikhism, this *Hukam* or Will may be understood to operate as internal to self. The expression Divine Reason seems to explain the concept of *Hukam* most appropriately. *Hukam* is not like an authoritarian external order. "It is within the man. It is a Divine Will which includes knowledge and that knowledge is reached through reason. Therefore, the expression may be called Divine Reason" (32). This idea is further stressed by Guru Nanak in *Sri Rag* (*Guru Granth Sahib*, M. 1, page 55). *Hukam* is the outstanding principle of the universe. Everything in nature is functioning according to set principles. Nothing is unprincipled. *Hukam* is the governing principle. Guru Arjan holds in *Sukhmani Sahib* (*Guru Granth Sahib*, M. 5, page 297), that *Hukam* is the invisible sustaining principle of this universe. God is the cause and creator of this universe and everything is created and destroyed through *Hukam*. The Guru further expresses that this coming and going in the world is only through *Hukam* (*Guru Granth Sahib*, M. 5, page 885).

Hukam, therefore, means the law of God, and it is not allowed to be evaluated. Guru Nanak says in *Japji pauri* 2 (morning prayer of the Sikhs): "Everyone is within His *Hukam* and there is no exception to this rule".

"In both happiness and sorrow one must thank Him. He is the saviour and the protector; He is the Giver and the Preserver. We, with our own actions, have to make ourselves worthy for His bounties and blessings. By accepting and revering His rules, and by living a life as ordained in His Law Book, one can make himself/herself worthy of His mercy and benevolence. His law is the ultimate justice and must be accepted without any groan" (33).

Karah Prasad: In order to remove untouchability, discourage caste system and maintain social equality, Guru Nanak started the practice of distributing *Karah Prasad* among the devotees. Even today, this practice continues in all the Gurdwaras across the country. The ingredients of *Karah Prasad* are water, flour (*atta*), clarified butter (*ghee*) and sugar. Besides these four material ingredients, *Karah Prasad* contains a spiritual ingredient Prayer (*Japji*), which is read while preparing it in a cauldron on fire. When it is ready, the *Karah Prasad* is placed on a small stool near the *Guru Granth Sahib*. When *Karah Prasad* is distributed in a Gurdwara, it is received by all without any distinction of caste or creed. "It is first cooked in an iron cauldron (*karaha*) and then a portion of it is distributed among the five beloved ones, who are known to have taken baptismal vows. Some quantity is also placed on a small stool near the *Adi Granth*. The rest is distributed among the devotees" (34).

Karah Prasad made out of water, flour (atta) clarified butter (ghee) and sugar is distributed in a Gurdwara among the devotees.

Celebrations: The Gurdwara celebrates the *Baisakhi* festival on a large scale, in mid-April every year. This festival is held on the first of the *Vikrami* month of *Baisakh*. A day before the first of *Baisakh*, in the year 1699 C.E., Guru Gobind Singh created the new order of the *Khalsa* at Anandpur. *Charanpahul* was replaced by *Khande da Amrit*. "This nector with steel, the Divine Word, and Guru's spirit dissolved in it, brought a miraculous change in the person who partook of it. The Guru abolished all distinctions of caste, creed and sex, and integrated his people into one homogenous fraternity" (35). Though the Guru introduced a new ideology, it was not a departure from the old ideals preached by Guru Nanak and his successors.

The Gurdwara also celebrates the birthday of Guru Hargobind who was born on June 14, 1595 C.E. at Wadali in Amritsar district. The celebration commemorates his gracious visit to this place before and after his incarceration in the Gwalior fort.

Of the ten historical Sikh Gurdwaras in Delhi, Gurdwara Majnu Tilla Sahib holds great significance not only because of its sanctification by the sacred visits of the two Gurus, but also because of its picturesque location on the banks of the river Yamuna.

Bangla Sahib

Historical background and associated myths and legends

Gurdwara Bangla Sahib is one of the most popular historical shrines in Delhi which attracts a good number of visitors and devotees everyday. The Gurdwara near Gole Market Post Office, adjacent to Connaught Place in New Delhi, marks the site of the Bungalow owned by Raja Jai Singh of Amber, where Guru Harkrishan stayed when summoned to Delhi by Emperor Aurangzeb. "In 1783 C.E. Sardar Baghel Singh is said to have established a Gurdwara here in memory of the young Guru's sacred visit. This was the area where Raja Jai Singh's armies were also stationed and was known as Jai Singhpura" (36).

Guru Har Rai had two sons, Ram Rai and Harkrishan. The younger Harkrishan succeeded to the *gaddi* in 1661 C.E. at the age of six.

As Ram Rai earned the displeasure of his father Guru Har Rai for giving a wrong interpretation of some of the hymns of *Guru Granth Sahib* in order to please Emperor Aurangzeb, he was not considered worthy of Guruship. When Ram Rai came to know that the crown of Guruship had been bestowed on his younger brother Harkrishan, he became so distressed that he prepared himself to fight for the spiritual leadership of the Sikh community with the help of all resources at hand. His followers, particularly the wily *Masand*s numbering about a hundred, only helped in inflaming his jealousy and injured vanity. With all his display of miracles (*Karamat*) and

Facing page: *An inside view of Gurdwara Bangla Sahib. The Gurdwara has a profusely decorated Prakash Asthan and a large hall for congregation.*

Pages 56-57: *Gurdwara Bangla Sahib located near Gole Market Post Office, adjacent to Connaught Place, New Delhi.*

his influence in the Delhi court, Ram Rai had failed to win over the leading Sikhs of Delhi and Punjab. Every Sikh knew that even in the past, the Guruship had always been bestowed on the most deserving member of the family, and not on the eldest son. Though Harkrishan was hardly six years old, he was deemed to be highly efficient and competent to guide the followers of Guru Nanak. He was a precocious child, a genius, and highly intellectual. Having had spiritual training, the young Harkrishan seemed like a perfect leader who could guide the Sikh community during one of the most critical periods of Sikh history, when Mughal Emperor Aurangzeb was in power.

As a last resort, Ram Rai approached Emperor Aurangzeb to help him to acquire the crown of Guruship. Prominent Sikhs of Delhi like Lakhi Rai, Kalyan Chand, the priest of the Delhi *Dharamsala*, Bhai Gurbaksh Mal, and the Sikh Missionary posted at Delhi, appealed to Ram Rai to desist from creating a new crisis by seeking the support of Emperor Aurangzeb. Ram Rai, instead of paying heed to their request, informed the Emperor that his followers would create trouble in Punjab if they were allowed to remain unchecked. Predictably, the Emperor summoned the child Guru Harkrishan to his court. Auragzeb thought if he could get Ram Rai the crown of Guruship, it would be easy to use him as a tool in his attempt to check the progress of the Sikhs under Guru Har Rai.

Guru Harkrishan, Eighth Guru of the Sikhs (1656–1664 C.E.) succeeded to the Gaddi in 1661 C.E. at the age of six.

When the Emperor's summons reached Kiratpur (ancestral home of Guru Harkrishan, district Ropar, Punjab), Guru Harkrishan refused to come to Delhi. The Sikhs of Delhi also did not like the idea of Guru

Harkrishan visiting Delhi. Fortunately both Raja Jai Singh of Amber, who was in the good books of the Emperor for his acumen, foresight and political cunning, and his son Ram Singh were in Delhi at that time. The Delhi Sikhs approached them to intervene and settle the issue at hand amicably. Raja Jai Singh took the responsibility of persuading the Guru to come to Delhi, but at the same time, also managed to get an assurance from the Emperor that as long as he was not satisfied about the succession issue, Guru Harkrishan would stay in his bungalow, as his guest. Aurangzeb readily agreed, as there was no political issue involved as such.

Raja Jai Singh sent a courtier named Diwan Paras Ram with valuable presents to Kiratpur to bring the Guru to Delhi. When the Guru reached Delhi he was received by Raja Jai Singh and his son Ram Singh in the most courteous and honourable manner. Guru Harkrishan was put up in their Bungalow at Raisina. However, Guru Harkrishan avoided meeting the Emperor and turned down all suggestions urging him to meet and impress upon the Mughal Emperor about the correctness of his father's decision regarding the succession issue. This bungalow where Guru Harkrishan stayed for a month or two became an important Sikh centre as hundreds of devotees used to visit the bungalow seeking his *darshan* everyday.

While Ram Rai was busy performing cheap miracles (*Karamat*) in the Mughal court and trying his best to influence the ministers with his usual gifts and to get Emperor Aurangzeb's order to oust Guru Harkrishan from the leadership of the Sikhs, the young Guru was busy performing the miracle of healing and giving solace to the sick and peace to the poor living in agonizing poverty. By serving the people irrespective of their caste or creed, the boy prophet won more adherents than any other religious leader living in Delhi at that time. The Muslims of Delhi were particularly impressed with the purity of his outlook and they nicknamed him 'Bala Pir' (child prophet). The stories of the young Guru's healing powers spread throughout the city, and it was known that even a glimpse of the Guru helped dispel sufferings. This is recorded later in history by Guru Gobind Singh:

> *Contemplate the spirit of Harkrishan,*
> *The sight of whom dispelleth all sorrow and suffering* (37).

Both the Hindus and the Muslims of Delhi followed the young prophet as a moth follows the flame. Emperor Aurangzeb's informers gave a very impressive report about the unusual powers and the magnetic personality of the young Guru. Raja Jai Singh was able to persuade the Emperor to leave the choice of selecting their spiritual leader to the Sikhs. Aurangzeb was, however, anxious to see the young Guru and Raja Jai Singh promised to fix a meeting.

In March, 1664 C.E., smallpox began to rage in the city of Delhi, in the form of an epidemic. The citizens of Delhi suffered grief and death as a result of this calamity. The young Guru stayed near the *Chubacha* (a reservoir of water) located at the bungalow complex out of love and compassion for those suffering. It is believed that all those who drank the Holy water from the *Chubacha* were cured of the disease. The people of Delhi were saved from the epidemic. Devotees with faith came from far and near and got rid of their suffering by taking the Holy water. The Guru moved among the poor, the sick and the destitute. He used to distribute succour, food, clothes and medicines to the sick. Unfortunately, though, amidst all this, the Guru himself suffered an attack of smallpox. As soon as the Mughal Emperor learnt that the Guru had an attack of smallpox, his proposed meeting with the Guru was cancelled. "On the fifth day of his illness, he told his mother that his end was approaching and he advised his followers to take him to the place (where the present Gurdwara Bala Sahib stands) on the bank of the river Yamuna" (38). As the Guru stayed in Raja Jai Singh's bungalow till the fourth day of his illness during his visit to Delhi, this bungalow later on became an important historical Sikh shrine, now known as Gurdwara Bangla Sahib.

A close view of the profusely decorated Prakash Asthan in Gurdwara Bangla Sahib.

Architectural details: An overview

Gurdwara Bangla Sahib is considered one of the popular and active historical Gurdwaras in Delhi. It marks the site of the bungalow owned by Raja Jai Singh of Amber. This Gurdwara, like other historical Gurdwaras of Delhi has been reconstructed and renovated over and over again. It has a spacious four-storey building with a beautiful façade.

The Gurdwara has a large hall for congregation. The hall has a profusely decorated *Prakash Asthan* with a provision for circumambulation (*Parikrama*). The walls, covered with marbles, are aesthetically carved with floral designs and motifs. The pillars too are covered by neat carvings, decorative designs and marbles. The doors of the building are decorated by exquisitely embossed silver sheets with variegated floral designs and motifs. The high-ceilinged hall has stairs at the rear portion of the building leading to the first floor where *Akhand Path*s are performed.

A panoramic view of Gurdwara Bangla Sahib; it has a spacious four storey building with a beautiful facade.

Just to the right of the entrance there is a *Chubacha* which is a perennial source of water. It is believed, till date, that this is the same *Chubacha* that cured masses suffering from smallpox with its Holy waters and that it is not only sacred, but also has healing powers.

In 1973, a fifteen metre deep new *Sarovar* was constructed in the Gurdwara complex based on the model of the *Sarovar* of the *Harimandir* in Amritsar, although not an exact copy.

Socio-cultural activities

The *Guru-ka-Langar* attached to the Gurdwara complex has the capacity to provide food for more than 1000 persons at a time. The Gurdwara offers four or five square meals everyday to all pilgrims, visitors, and the poor and destitutes of the city. The *Guru-ka-Langar* here is considered to be one of the busiest of all *Guru-ka-Langar*s.

The service begins from 12.30 a.m. and continues upto 10 p.m. Just opposite the *Guru-ka-Langar*, a large guesthouse has been constructed for providing accommodation for the pilgrims and travellers.

Gurdwara Bangla Sahib's museum has earned the distinction of having in its possession a unique collection of paintings and manuscripts. Named after Sardar Baghel Singh, the museum has been established by the Delhi Sikh Gurdwara Management Committee to commemorate the historical victory of Delhi by the *Khalsa* and to acknowledge Sardar Baghel Singh's unique contribution in erecting Sikh shrines in Delhi.

The collection of the manuscripts includes the following:

- Manusript *Sukhmani Sahib* (hand written).
- Old Manuscript *Gurbani Guru Gobind Singh Ji.*
- Old Manuscript *Pothi Sahib Guru Nanak Bani*, 1876 C.E.
- *Suraj Prakash* (life of Guru Tegh Bahadur Ji) by Bhai Santokh Singh Churamani, 1878 C.E. (hand written).
- Old Manuscript *Janam Sakhi Baba Nanak* (by Bhai Bala) with Old Manuscript *Japji Sahib* by Anand Ghan Udasi, 1865 C.E.
- Old Manuscript *Guru Nanak Prakash* by Bhai Santokh Singh (life of Sri Guru Nanak).
- *Gurbilas Guru Hargobind Sahib Ji* by Kavi Sohan, 1866 C.E.

The paintings of portraits of the Gurus and other Sikh leaders and personalities and the paintings depicting various events in the history of the Sikhs, appear to be very important resource materials for the study of Sikh history and religion. The paintings depict Guru Nanak's visit to Baghdad in 1518 C.E., his visit to Sri Lanka, his meeting with Babur at Eminabad in 1520 C.E. and his visit to Multan. Among other important paintings, mention may be made of the depictions of Emperor Akbar in the presence of Guru Amar Das; construction of the tank of nectar, *Amrit Sarovar* in 1577 C.E.; martyrdom of Sri Guru Arjan (30 May, 1606 C.E.); Sri Guru Harkrishan Sahib's trampling the arrogance of a

Brahmin Chandu Lal and his enthralling a poor water carrier named *Chhajju* to recite the *Gita*; Guru Harkrishan's giving succour to all in distress during the smallpox epidemic in Delhi; Guru Teg Bahadur promising all help and protection to a delegation of 500 Brahmins and Kashmiri supplicants in 1675 C.E.; Guru Tegh Bahadur's martyrdom and Bhai Jaita and Bhai Lakhi Shah Vanjara's acts of bravery after Guru Tegh Bahadur's martyrdom; the Battle of Bhangani (Paonta Sahib, April, 1687 C.E.); the fortress at Chamkaur (December 22, 1704 C.E.); the younger *Sahibzada*s with their grandmother Mata Gujri in the Cold Tower (*Thanda Burj*; December 26, 1704 C.E.); Trial of Dallay (1706 C.E.); a unique procession of Banda Singh Bahadur and his brave soldiers (1716 C.E.); martyrdom of Baba Banda Singh Bahadur (June 19, 1716 C.E.); martyrdom of Sikhs at Lahore (1753 C.E.); Sikh march to Bikaner; Sikhs freeing Indian women enslaved by Ahmad Shah Abdali (1762 C.E.); Sardar Baghel Singh Ji entering Delhi (March 11 1781 C.E.); Sikhs capturing the Red Fort at Delhi (March 11, 1781 C.E.), and the sacrifice at Panja Sahib (October 30, 1922 C.E.).

The daily programmes of the Gurdwara are more or less similar across all other historical Gurdwaras of Delhi. Starting with *Prakash* in the early morning hours, the day's programme includes, among others, the recitations/singing of *Sukhmani Sahib, Nitnem, Asa-di-Var, Japji, Anand Sahib, Rehras, Aarti Kirtan, Kirtan Sohila* and *Guru itihas katha* followed by *Ardas, Hukamnama* and *Prasad*. Besides routine prayers and celebration of usual anniversaries (*Gurpurbs*), the Gurdwara especially celebrates the birth anniversary of Guru Harkrishan in the month of July-August. Thousands of visitors and devotees come to pay homage to the child Guru and observe the day's programmes with great enthusiasm.

Other relevant information

Among the ancillary buildings located in the Gurdwara complex, the following execute social welfare activities:

- Guru Harkrishan Hospital: It runs a Charitable Out Patients' Department (O.P.D) from morning till noon that offers treatments for various ailments in case of emergency.
- A reference library for those who want to study Sikh history and religion.
- A sales counter for publications on Sikh history and religion.

As Gurdwara Bangla Sahib is located in the heart of the capital city, the number of visitors to this sacred shrine is obviously more than the number of visitors to other historical Gurdwaras in Delhi. Even the total number of foreign visitors to this Gurdwara in a year, as roughly calculated on the basis of daily entries in registers, is about 50,000. As reported by the Information Officer, the maximum number of foreign visitors are from France.

Keeping in view the number of visitors and devotees to this Gurdwara everyday, the concerned authorities have constructed a large parking complex just opposite to the main entrance of the shrine.

ਅੰਗੀਠਾ

Bala Sahib

Historical background and associated myths and legends

Gurdwara Bala Sahib is considered one of the most sacred historical shrines in Delhi. It was here that the young Guru Harkrishan was cremated after he breathed his last on March 30, 1664 C.E. This place is also most revered because both Mata Sundari and Mata Sahib Devan (the holy mothers and devoted wives of Guru Gobind Singh) were cremated here, and their *Samadhi*s are also preserved in the compound of this Gurdwara.

Located between Mathura Road and the bend of Ring Road and near Nizamuddin Railway Station and village Kilokri in South Delhi, this Gurdwara commemorates the sacred memory of Guru Harkrishan, who died here in a tent erected for his stay on the fifth day of his serious illness.

Guru Harkrishan's last rites were performed where the present Gurdwara Bala Sahib (named after his nickname "Bala Pir") has been built. His ashes were taken to his birth place at Kiratpur Sahib (located on the banks of river Satlej near Anandpur Sahib in the Ropar district, Punjab), where they were preserved with respect and devotion in an urn at Patalpuri (also at Kiratpur Sahib), the place where Guru Hargobind breathed his last. Before his death, the child Guru told everyone including his mother not to mourn his death. As willed by the Guru, there were no lamentations, no cries, no sobbings, but only chantings of the sacred hymns and the recitation of the Lord's name (*Nam*).

Facing page: *Memorial (Samadhi) raised over the ashes of Mata Sundarji who was cremated here in the Bala Sahib Gurdwara complex.*

Pages 68-69: *A general view of Gurdwara Bala Sahib located between Mathura Road and the bend of Ring Road in South Delhi. This Gurdwara was constructed on the spot where Guru Harkrishan died in a tent erected for his stay on the fifth day of his serious illness.*

"The Gurus exhorted their followers to earn their living through hardwork (Kirt Karo), share the fruit of their labour with others (Vand Chhako) and recite and follow God's Nam (Nam Japo)" (39).

There are two types of God's names—the Attributive name which describes the power of God, and the True Name which emanates from the Guru's personal experience and vision of the Divine Being. The Name is contemplated and repeated in the inner consciousness of deep meditation. "The True Name in the deeper sense is not the word by which we describe an object, but the total power, quality, character of reality in which the Prophet has tried to sum up the mystic power and the experience of His presence. The True Name is the embodiment of His power, His light, His wisdom"(40).

In the name, the Lord's spirit abides,
May the name in me be dwelling.
Without the Guru we walk in darkness;
Without the Word we understand not life.
The Word of the Guru is light.
His Word's light leads to Truth (41).

Architectural details: An overview

The Bala Sahib Gurdwara was first built by Sardar Baghel Singh during his stay in Delhi in 1783 C.E. Its present building has been thoroughly reconstructed by Late Baba Harbans Singh a couple of years ago. The architecture of the building is almost similar to that of other historical shrines in Delhi, which have also been reconstructed by Late Baba Harbans Singh. One of the main attractions of the building complex is a separate memorial (*Samadhi*) raised over the ashes of Mata Sundariji who was cremated here. The memorial raised over the ashes of Mata Sahib Devan, who was also cremated here, now forms a part of the main building which is visible on the right side of the main entrance of the Gurdwara building.

Facing Page: *Prakash Asthan located inside the building of the Gurdwara Bala Sahib.*

ਸ੍ਰੀ ਹਰਿਕ੍ਰਿਸ਼ਨ
ਡਿਠ ਸਭਿ ਦੁਖ ਜਾਇ ॥

Socio-cultural activities

The Gurdwara celebrates birthdays of Guru Nanak and Guru Gobind Singh, and observes martyrdom (*shahidi*) of Guru Arjan Dev (fifth Guru) and Guru Tegh Bahadur (ninth Guru). The main celebration is, however, *Jyoti Jot Gurpurb* related to Guru Harkrishan's life. The celebration is arranged for a day in the month of April every year. It attracts a good number of visitors and devotees from the nearby localities and also from the South Delhi areas.

The Gurdwara has undertaken the construction of a 400-bed hospital in its compound with a view to provide necessary medical aids to the people, irrespective of caste, creed, religion and nationality. The project had been sponsored by Late Baba Harbans Singh Karsevawale. There is a 50-bed hospital (named after Guru Harkrishan), and a dispensary within the Gurdwara complex. Apart from payment of a token donation, the outpatients are not required to pay any amount for their treatment and medicines. The patients usually come from nearby localities, especially from the adjoining Kilokri village and a considerable percentage of them belong to the Muslim community.

The *Guru–ka-Langar* (attached to the Gurdwara complex) plays an important role in maintaining social equality in this Gurdwara. Even today, the people must be remembering that, "The young Guru who decided to take the suffering of the people on his own person, had an attack of smallpox. Many people had been cured by the tender care he bestowed on them, but for him the disease was symbolic of God's Will that he should cast away his body. The young Guru lived with all his superhuman gifts and powers in a natural way and he wanted to cast off the body in a natural way" (42).

Other relevant information

According to the local residents of the area, the Gurdwara complex had an old well and an old pipal tree within its precincts till 1986. With time, these two examples of cultural and environmental heritage fell prey to renovation/reconstruction within the Gurdwara complex. The only surviving example of cultural heritage is the tower known as *Baba-Bir-Singh-ki-Gumti*, located in front of D Block staff quarter, attached to the Gurdwara complex. Baba Bir Singh appears to have been a devout follower of Sikhism. His stay in this *Gumti* reveals his great respect for the child Guru.The double-storeyed round-shaped tower (*Gumti*) of moderate height, has separate entrances for the ground and the upper floor. The ground floor of the *Gumti* is, however, in the occupation of a staff member of the Delhi Sikh Gurdwara Management Committee. Though the tower is in a good condition, it is important that necessary steps are initiated by the Delhi Sikh Gurdwara Management Committee for its upkeep.

Sis Ganj Sahib

Historical background and associated myths and legends

Gurdwara Sis Ganj Sahib is considered to be one of the most sacred historical shrines for the reason that it is a monument dedicated to the martyrdom of Guru Tegh Bahadur, who, in the words of Guru Gobind Singh (Tenth Guru of the Sikhs), gave away his life for the protection of the religious symbols of the Hindus. The Guru was beheaded here publically on November 11, 1675 C.E. Writing about his predecessor and illustrious father's martyrdom, Guru Gobind Singh wrote in *Bachiter Natak*:

> *Guru Tegh Bahadur broke his earthly*
> *vessel on Aurangzeb's head.*
> *And went to the Home of God.*
> *No one had ever performed such a noble act,*
> *like the self-sacrifice of Guru Tegh Bahadur.*
> *When Guru Tegh Bahadur passed away,*
> *The world was sorrow stricken;*
> *Alas! Alas! Rose the wailing cries on earth;*
> *The shouts of Glory! Glory, resounded in heaven(43).*

Guru Tegh Bahadur, the Ninth Guru of the Sikhs (1621-1675 C.E.) who gave away his life for the protection of the religious symbols of the Hindus.

The Muhgal Emperor Aurangzeb's reign was marked by the persecution of the Hindus, as he followed a policy of religious intolerance. He appointed *Mullah*s to check on all ostentatious display of idol worship. He also forbade fairs during Hindu festivals, and had driven out large number of *Yogi*s, *Sanyasi*s and other religious souls out of his dominions.

Aurangzeb was told by his advisors, *Maulvi*s and *Ulema*s that if he wanted to convert 'Dar-ul-herb' into 'Dar-ul-Islam', he should first convert the Brahmins of the country, as they were the exponents of the Hindu religion. Once they are converted, it would be easy to establish 'Dar-ul-Islam' in the country. Aurangzeb was convinced, and he issued orders that the Brahmins of Kashmir, Kashi, Prayag, Kurukshetra and Haridwar be converted with lightening speed. In his pursuit, Aurangzeb put hundreds of Brahmins into jail. In accordance with the Emperor's order, Sher Afghan Khan (Iftikhar Khan), the then Viceroy in Kashmir, tyrannized over the Brahmins to such an extent that it is said he sent bundles of the sacred thread worn by the Brahmins to the Emperor, whom, he either converted, or killed.

The troubled Brahmins of North India are said to have appealed to some Hindu leaders, but they expressed their helplessness. Ultimately, about 500 Brahmins representing various centres of learning, from Banaras to Srinagar, under the leadership of Pandit Kripa Ram proceeded to Anandpur where Guru Tegh Bahadur, the Ninth Guru, was then residing. They were hopeful that their honour and faith could be protected by Guru Tegh Bahadur as he strongly believed in the freedom of worship for all.

When the persecuted Brahmins arrived at Anandpur, the Guru was addressing the *Darbar*. When the Guru finished his sermon, Kripa Ram appeared before him and apprised the Guru of the atrocities committed on them by Aurangzeb's Governor, Iftikhar Khan, in Kashmir. The Guru gave him a patient hearing, listening to the horrific tales of torture and suffering of the Hindus, and the forcible conversion of women, men and even boys. The Guru was visibly moved by the woeful tales of the Brahmins.

Page 78: *Just below the Prakash Asthan of the prayer hall, there is small room in the basement which is meant for preserving the exact holy spot where Guru Tegh Bahadur sacrificed his life. This room is also used as a Prakash Asthan where the Guru Granth Sahib is seated.*

Pages 76-77: *A general view of Gurdwara Sis Ganj Sahib. The building represents somewhat a different type of architecture as compared to other historical Gurdwaras of Delhi.*

Encouraged by his young son, Gobind, Guru Tegh Bahadur advised the *Pandit*s to go to Emperor Aurnagzeb and tell him that they, together with all the Brahmins were ready to embrace Islam, if Tegh Bahadur, who was their Guru, was first converted. The Guru also advised them to present their petition to the Emperor through the Governor of Lahore.

Pandit Kripa Ram and his associates sent a petition through Zalim Khan, the then Governor of Lahore, to Aurangzeb saying that if he succeeded in converting Guru Tegh Bahdur, they would all accept Islam. The Emperor was highly gratified to read the petition. He then issued summons from Agra for the Guru to present himself in his court. He ordered four officers to proceed to Anandpur and hand over the Emperor's order to the Guru. The Guru sent a reply to the Emperor saying that he would come to Delhi of his own accord, after the monsoons.

It was in the month of June, 1675 C.E., that the Guru set out for Delhi along with his five devotees, Bhai Mati Das, Bhai Sati Das, Bhai Dayal Das, Bhai Udhe and Bhai Gurditta. "When the Guru was on the way to Delhi, he sent for his youthful son, and girding upon him the sword of Guru Hargobind, he hailed him as the Guru of the Sikhs. He told him he was himself being led to death, he counselled him not to leave his body a prey to dogs, and he enjoined upon him the necessity and the merit of revenge"(44). The Guru halted at several places en route to Delhi from Anandpur, and that delayed his journey. Aurangzeb became impatient. The *Qazi*s and *Mullah*s made him believe that the Guru was trying to escape from coming in to Delhi. Without delay, Aurangzeb sent two trusted emissaries to Anandpur to find the Guru and bring him to Delhi. These persons even went to Amritsar and several other places to trace the Guru, but they failed in their mission. They reported to Aurangzeb that the Guru was absconding and on hearing this, Aurangzeb issued warrants for his arrest.

On the other hand, the Guru continued on his journey to Delhi. He first went to Agra in the hope of meeting the Emperor there, but

Facing Page Top: *A painting showing Bhai Moti Das (a companion of Guru Tegh Bahadur) being cut in twain with a saw.*

Facing Page Centre: *A painting showing how Bhai Dayal Das (another disciple of Guru Tegh Bahadur) was thrown into a cauldron of boiling water. He bore the brutal suffering without a murmur.*

Facing Page Bottom: *Emperor Aurangzeb directed that Guru Tegh Bahadur be imprisoned in a small iron cage. The painting shows Guru Tegh Bahadur imprisoned in a small cage where he was subjected to severe torture for several days.*

Below: *A painting showing how Bhai Sati Das (a companion of Guru Tegh Bahadur) was wrapped all around with cotton, and then set on fire.*

the Emperor was in Delhi. In the fort of Agra, the Guru was told that since the Emperor had already left for Delhi, the Guru would also be taken there and Aurangzeb was informed about the arrest of the Guru. Delighted, Aurangzeb ordered that the Guru be immediately brought to Delhi.

However, there is a contradiction regarding Aurangzeb's date of arrival in Delhi. Earlier scholars namely J.D. Cunnigham and Dr. Trilochan Singh are of the view that Aurangzeb reached Delhi sometime in the middle of 1675 C.E. Recent researches, however, reveal that Aurangzeb was away from Delhi and Agra from March, 1674 C.E. to December, 1675 C.E. He reached Delhi only on March 27, 1676 C.E. In the book titled *History of The Sikhs And Their Religion*, edited by Kirpal Singh and Kharak Singh, and published by Shiromani Gurdwara Prabandhak Committee, Amritsar, 2004, Surjit Singh Gandhi in his chapter on Nanak IX-Guru Tegh Bahadur has stated on the basis of available evidence that Aurangzeb left Delhi for Hasan Abdal on April 17, 1674 C.E. and reached there on June 26, 1674 C.E. The emperor aimed at restoring the Imperial writ in the Pathan land from Kandahar to Attock where different tribes had defied the Mughal authority, and had risen in open revolt against it. Aurangzeb stayed there from June 1674 C.E. to December, 1675 C.E. He left Lahore on February 24, 1676 C.E., and reached Delhi on March 27, 1676 C.E. That the emperor was not physically present at the time of Guru Tegh Bahadur's martyrdom has also been proved by the positive evidence of *Máasir-i-Alamgiri* written by Saqi Mastan Khan serving in the administration of Aurangzeb. The dates of Aurangzeb's itinerary as stated above are also corroborated by *Máasir-i-Alamgiri.*

Though the Emperor was not present in Delhi, he ordered that the Guru be imprisoned in a small iron cage and brought to Delhi. Accordingly, cast in an iron cage the Guru was taken to Delhi on November 4, 1675 C.E. He was put in chains and ordered to be tortured until he would accept Islam. The emperor's ministers and the Chief *Qazi* also tried their best to persuade the Guru to accept Islam, but the Guru refused. The Emperor also ordered that, if the Guru refused to obey his order, his devoted followers were to be tortured to death in his presence. He did this with the belief that the Guru would get terrified on seeing these horific scenes and would embrace Islam.

Next day Guru Tegh Bahadur's companions, (except Bhai Udhe and Bhai Gurditta who were asked by the Guru to leave the place) Bhai Mati Das, Bhai Sati Das and Bhai Dayal Das were tortured to death. The body of Moti Das was cut in twain with a saw and Dayal Das was thrown into a cauldron of boiling water. Sati Das was wrapped all around with cotton and then set on fire. Their bodies were cut to pieces and displayed in public. This was done with a clear motive of showing the champions of the freedom-of-worship movement, the extent of grievous torture that they may have to undergo. When the Guru could not be persuaded to abandon his religious faith, he was asked to perform some miracle *(Karamat)* to prove the divinity of his mission. This also he declined, saying that it was never right for any one to try to intervene in the Will of God.

When all attempts to persuade the Guru to accept Islam failed, the Emperor ordered that the Guru be executed in public at Chandni Chowk.

Then came the fateful day. It was Thursday, November 11, 1675 C.E. The Guru was taken out of his iron cage. He was allowed to perform his ablutions at a well nearby. After that, the Guru sat under a banyan tree and started reciting *Japji*. The Guru was then brought to the open space where the executioner, Jallaluddin of Samana, stood with a drawn sword ready to act at his master's order. The vast gathering of people stood motionless with irate feelings. The Guru blessed them, and, raising his hands, consoled them. Tears welled up in the masses' eyes and they shut their eyes to avoid witnessing the horror unfolding before them.

A few moments passed. The executioner waved his sword and cut off the Guru's head. The mutilated body was left in Chandni Chowk unattended and none dared claim it for fear of Mughal reprisal. At nightfall, the severed head of the Guru was lifted by Bhai Jaita, a Rangreta, a low caste who secretly carried it to Anandpur for cremation. It is said that a great storm hit the city that day and filled everyone's eyes with dust. The whole of Delhi was struck with terror. Some cried in utter helplessness, some screamed and beat their chests out of unbearable agony and remorse. "Thus the Guru fell a victim to the religious bigotry of the then ruler of the land and sacrificed his life for protecting the sacred marks of the Hindus, for freedom of conscience and worship, and for the sake of dharma, righteousness"(46).

Writing about the martyrdom of his illustrious father, Guru Gobind Singh said in *Bachiter Natak*:

He sacrificed his life,
For protecting the rights of Hindus,
To wear sacred thread and caste symbols;
He made the supreme sacrifice in this dark age,
He gave his head, but did not utter a word in pain.
He suffered martyrdom for the sake of dharma,
He did this great heroic deed.
He readily gave up his head,
But did not give up his conviction.
He avoided performing miracles,
A cheap act of fooling people,
For such acts men of God are ashamed (47).

History is full of tales of martyrs who were first arrested and then executed by the people in power, whom they opposed or resisted for a righteous cause. But Guru Tegh Bahadur's martyrdom was unique and an unparalled incident in the history of mankind in the sense that he came to Delhi from Anandpur on his own and sacrificed his life for saving a religion in which he himself did not believe, and which he tried to reform. In the words of Dr. Indubhushan Banerjee, "The Guru's was thus a self-sought martyrdom, a willing sacrifice for religion. Knowing fully well the might of the Emperor and his own comparative helplessness, he yet took up the cause of the persecuted Hindus. His offence, in the Emperor's eyes, was thus exceedingly serious and it is no wonder that he met his death in execution"(48).

On the site where Guru Tegh Bahadur was martyred, stands Gurdwara Sis Ganj Sahib. It is located in Chandni Chowk, the most prosperous business centre of Delhi. The trunk of the pipal tree under which the Guru was martyred has been preserved. The well from which the Guru took water for his bath while in prison and before his martyrdom still exists in the same place.

Architectural details: An overview

The sacred place where the martyrdom of Guru Teg Bahadur took place had fallen into oblivion till 1783 C.E. On March 9, 1783 C.E., the Sikhs under the leadership of Jassa Singh Ramgarhia, Baghel Singh Karorsinghia and Rai Singh Bhangi advanced to the Imperial Capital (*Delhi Chronicle 350-351*) and attacked the Red Fort. As this sudden attack created panic in the city, the Delhi Court opened negotiations. The Sikhs received cash worth three lakhs and the permission to build their historic shrines in Delhi. Because of the sudden death of Jassa Singh Ahluwalia, the founder of the Ahluwalia *Misl* and the leader of *Dal Khalsa*, the *Misl* Sardars invited Jassa Singh Ramgarhia to Punjab. "Baghel Singh Karorsinghia remained at Delhi as the head of four thousand Sikh troops to build historical shrines at the places, sanctified

An inner view of Gurdwara Sis Ganj Sahib showing Prakash Asthan and a hall for congregration.

by the visits of the Gurus, specially where Guru Tegh Bahadur was martyred"(49). It may be presumed that no Sikh shrine was erected at the place of Guru Tegh Bahadur's martyrdom during the period between 1675 C.E. and 1783 C.E. It is, however, believed that Guru Gobind Singh identified the exact sites in Delhi sanctified by the visits and martyrdoms of the Sikh Gurus, during his stay in Delhi in 1707 C.E. The sites demarcated by erecting *Nishan Sahib* (Sikh flag) were Guru Nanak Piau, Majnu Tilla, Bangla Sahib, Bala Sahib, Sis Ganj and Rakab Ganj. In the course of time, these sacred sites metamorphosed into mosques. On-the-spot enquiry by Sardar Baghel Singh, however, revealed the fact that at the place of the pipal tree under which Guru Tegh Bahadur was martyred, a mosque had been built. Sardar Baghel Singh undertook the demolition of the mosque. As the work was being carried speedily, thousands of Muslims appeared on the scene to protect the mosque. The Sikhs under the leadership of Sardar Baghel

Singh faced them most courageously and chased them away. When the matter was reported to the Mughal Emperor Shah Alam II, he told the Muslims that the Sikhs had agreed to leave Delhi only on his assurance that all their sacred historical sites connected with the sacred visits of their Gurus would be restored to them for building Gurdwaras in these places, and that he had to fulfil his promise. As desired by the king, Sadat Ali Khan, who was the leader of the people putting obstacles in the demolition of the mosque, agreed to the Sikhs' right to build a Gurdwara at the place of Guru Tegh Bahadur's martyrdom. "The Emperor was also good enough to grant the Gurdwara a Jagir of Rs 4,000 from Pipli village. When Sardar Baghel Singh left for Punjab, this Gurdwara was demolished by the Muslim fanatics to build a mosque on the site"(50).

It was in 1857 C.E., when the uprising of the Sepoy Mutiny was crushed by the British, that Raja Sarup Singh of Jind, a devout follower of Sikhism, obtained permission to demolish the mosque and reconstruct a Gurdwara there. However, some Muslims moved the Calcutta High Court and obtained a decree and again demolished the Gurdwara. Finally, Raja Ranbir Singh of Jind took the matter to the Privy Council which gave a verdict in favour of the Sikhs. The mosque was demolished and a Gurdwara building came up in 1861 C.E.

The present building which replaced the older one during the 1930's is a multi-storeyed imposing edifice, topped by a golden-domed pavilion in the centre and domed kiosks on the corners. Besides the main Gurdwara building, there used to be a *Kotwali* where the Guru was held captive. The *Kotwali* was transformed into the *Guru-ka-Langar* and a *Sarai* in the year 1980.

The present building of the Gurdwara represents somewhat a different type of architecture as compared to the other historical Gurdwaras of Delhi.

The prayer hall is quite spacious with a number of ceiling fans provided for the devotees' comfort. The hall has a number of heavily

carved pillars and a number of doors on all sides facilitating easy entrance for the visitors. Just below the *Prakash Asthan* of the prayer hall, there is a small room in the basement which is meant for preserving the exact holy spot where Guru Tegh Bahadur sacrificed his life. This room is also used as a *Prakash Asthan* where the *Guru Granth Sahib* is seated. The trunk of the tree under which the Guru was executed is still preserved in the Gurdwara. The 'well' where he bathed before his execution is in good shape till today.

The facade of the *Guru-ka-Langar* building is so well decorated, it is difficult to imagine that it was originally a *Kotwali* where the Guru*ji* was held captive in an iron cage.

Social and cultural activities

The Gurdwara appears to be one of the most active historical shrines in Delhi. It is visited by thousands of devotees every day. The devotees come from different parts of the country especially Punjab.

The daily programmes of the Gurdwara start with *Prakash* from 2.30 a.m. Among the daily programmes, special mention may be made of the recitations of the *Bani*s from *Sukhmani Sahib, Nitnem, Asa-di-Var, Japji, Anand Sahib, Rehras, Aarti kirtan* and *Kirtan Sohila* followed by *Ardas, Hukamnama* and *Prasad*. The prayer hall is always found busy in holding congregational worship (*Sangat*).

The *Guru-ka-Langar* offers three square meals to all pilgrims and visitors. The total number of people who partake food in the *Guru-ka-Langar* every day is estimated to be about 3,000. Apart from the *Guru-ka-Langar* service, the Gurdwara also provides food to the pilgrims who come in at odd hours or stay in the residential premises of the Gurdwara complex.

The Gurdwara celebrates most of the important *Gurpurb*s, specially the birthdays of Guru Nanak and Guru Tegh Bahadur, and martyrdom of Guru Arjan Dev and Guru Tegh Bahadur. *Baisakhi* is celebrated in the month of April in a big way.

Page 88-89: *A panoramic night view of the recently inaugurated Guru Tegh Bahadur Memorial on the G.T. Karnal Road near Singhu Border.*

Facing page: *A view of the Guru Tegh Bahadur Memorial. This image shows Delhi Chief Minister Sheila Dikshit, Congress General Secretary Rahul Gandhi, and DSGMC President Sardar Paramjit Singh Sarna on the day of its inauguration.*

The Gurdwara houses an excellent reference library and a sales counter for publications on Sikh history and religion, published in English, Hindi and Punjabi. It also runs a senior secondary school named Guru Tegh Bahadur Khalsa Girls Senior School.

To pay homage to the memory of Guru Tegh Bahadur, Delhi Tourism and Transportation Development Corporation of the Delhi Government has recently inaugurated a memorial dedicated to Guru Tegh Bahadur. An architectural marvel, the memorial gives an insight into the life and teachings of the ninth Guru of the Sikhs. Constructed in an area of 11.87 acres along the National Highway I (G.T. Karnal Road) near Singhu Border, the memorial would be known for its architecture, design and world-class illumination. The memorial also has a unique concept. The 24-metre high central pylon made of stainless steel represents Guru Tegh Bahadur, while the three 15-metre high semi-arches represent his three disciples. Ten monoliths (11 to 18 metres tall) around it represent ten Sikh Gurus, and disseminate their teachings. The monoliths are inscribed with fundamental tenets of Sikhism translated in four languages—Hindi, English, Punjabi and Urdu.

Rakab Ganj Sahib

Historical background and associated myths and legends

This is the most sacred shrine of the Sikhs because it was here that the headless body of Guru Tegh Bahadur was cremated after his martyrdom. It is the place where the ashes of the great master were put in a copper urn and buried. Every visitor or devotee while visiting this Gurdwara pays homage to this spiritual ruler of the Sikhs, 'Sacha Padshah'—the true king.

After the martyrdom of Guru Tegh Bahadur, his body lay unattended in a dungeon for sometime in the darkness of that fateful night. When the clouds darkened, and the storm was raging furiously, a devotee of the Guru, named Lakhi Shah, a royal contractor, came to the dungeon with his eight sons and a large convoy of bullocks, carts, camels and horses.

They covered the body under heavy cotton bales in a cart and carried it to their residence at Raisina village which had many thatched cottages. The body was kept in one of these cottages which was set on fire. "After the fire was extinguished, they picked up the remains of the Guru and placing them in the copper urn buried them at the very spot where Guruji was cremated"(51).

The sacred place where the Gurdwara stands today used to be the residence of the Emperor's bodyguards during the Mughal period. There was a store house at this place for *Rakab*s (stirrups) from which the Gurdwara derives its name, Rakab Ganj.

Facing page: *Inner view of Gurdwara Rakab Ganj Sahib showing the Prakash Asthan where Guru Granth Sahib is seated under a gold-plated canopy.*

Pages 92-93: *A panoramic view of Gurdwara Rakab Ganj Sahib located near President's Estate, Central Secretariat and Parliament House, New Delhi. The Gurdwara is located at the spot where Bhai Lakhi Shah cremated Guru Tegh Bahadur's headless body by setting his house on fire.*

Architectural details: An overview

The sacred spot where Guru Tegh Bahadur's body was cremated fell into oblivion till it was located by Sardar Baghel Singh Karorsinghia in 1783 C.E.

During his visit to the site of the cremation, Baghel Singh saw a mosque already built there. The matter was reported to Emperor Shah Alam II who had accorded permission to Sardar Baghel Singh to build shrines at those places in the city sanctified by the visits of the Gurus. When the news of the impending demolition of the mosque spread all over Delhi, scores of Muslims assembled near the mosque. Baghel Singh proposed a way of reconciliation to the enraged Muslim masses. He suggested to them that, on digging up the place, if a copper urn containing the ashes of Guru Tegh Bahadur together with a nine-inch sword was found, the mosque would be converted into a Gurdwara. However, if that was not found, the mosque would continue to exist. When the earth was dug, a copper urn along with a nine-inch sword was found. This was enough to convince the Muslims, and a Gurdwara was constructed at the sight. "Baghel Singh also got a big Jagir attached to the Gurdwara"(52).

At the time of the Sepoy Mutiny in 1857 C.E., the Muslims once again demolished the Gurdwara and replaced it by a mosque. The Sikhs took the matter to the High Court and later to the Privy Council. The case was decided in their favour and a Gurdwara building was constructed at the site again.

In early March, 1914 C.E., a dispute arose between the Sikhs and the Government of India regarding the boundary wall of the Gurdwara. The government pulled down a portion of its wall because it stood in the way of a road to be constructed. Great resistance was offered by the Sikhs and a *morcha* was launched, but it was suspended during the First World War. However, the issue was again taken up after the war by Sardar Harchand Singh and Master Sundar Singh of Lyallpur (now in Pakistan), and Sardar Sardul Singh Caveeshar of Lahore. As

A general view of Gurdwara Rakab Ganj Sahib.

the government refused to respect the sentiments of the Sikhs, they decided to send a *shahidi jatha* (a batch of martyrs), to rebuild the demolished wall and face the consequences. The government realized the seriousness of the situation. Before the *jatha* arrived in Delhi, "Maharaja Ripudaman Singh of Nabha (the capital of erstwhile Nabha state, district Patiala, Punjab) arranged for the reconstruction of the wall on behalf of the Government of India"(53). The Maharaja, who had shown sympathy for the nationalist elements fighting for the liberation of the Gurdwaras from the control of the *Mahant*s, was asked by the government to take necessary steps for reconstruction.

The present building of Gurdwara Rakab Ganj is a magnificent, compact, multi-storeyed marble structure. It is important to note here that a single devotee named Sardar Harnam Singh Suri constructed this edifice by spending all the savings he had during his lifetime. He is said to have started the construction work in the year 1967, and got the work completed within a span of 15 years. The frontage on all the four sides of the building is the same with several steps leading to the hall where congregations are held. Pyramidal in design and built on a raised plinth, the building is decorated with rich architectural embellishments. Several domes, some big, some small, adorn the compact structure. The massive gateway to the Gurdwara is also an impressive structure.

It deserves special mention in this context that the architecture of the historical shrines of Delhi including that of Gurdwara Rakab Ganj represents a combination of the age-old Hindu and Muslim artistic traditions. It is in fact, more than a mere combination of the two, and, marks the beginning of a new and innovatory temple architecture in the country.

Located in the heart of the city, just opposite the Parliament House, Gurdwara Rakab Ganj is visited by innumerable devotees and visitors throughout the year. The visitors come from all parts of the country. A visit to the Rakab Ganj Gurdwara is in fact deemed to be a pilgrimage of sorts, which all true devotees treasure and like to go back to time and again.

The *Prakash Asthan* where the *Guru Granth Sahib* is seated under a gold plated canopy, is located just above the exact spot where the headless body of Guru Tegh Bahdur was cremated by Lakhi Shah's sons.

The *Samadhi* of Guru Tegh Bahadur is marked by a *Akhand jyoti*, and a *Kirpan* and a seal-symbol (containing a *Kalgi*—a crescent mark) originally belonging to Guru Tegh Bahadur and Guru Gobind Singh. The blood-stained *chola* (cloak) which Guru Tegh Bahadur was wearing before his martyrdom at Sis Ganj, was carried by Lakhi Shah's sons along with the headless body of the Guru. It is believed that the *chola* was taken out at the time of bathing the Guru's body before his cremation and preserved in their house. Guru Gobind Singh visited the *Samadhi* of Guru Tegh Bahadur during his stay

A view of Gurdwara Rakab Ganj Sahib at night.

in Delhi in 1707 C.E. He demarcated the exact site of Guru Tegh Bahadur's memorial and erected a Sikh flag (*Nishan Sahib*) as the essential distinguishing feature of the Guru's *Samadhi*. During his visit to the sacred memorial, Lakhi Shah's family members gave Guru Gobind Singh the *chola* which was in their custody, but Guru Gobind Singh advised them to keep it with them.

When Sardar Baghel Singh built a Gurdwara over the *Samadhi* of Guru Tegh Bahadur in 1783 C.E., Lakhi Shah's family members once again approached Sardar Baghel Singh to take care of the *chola* but Sardar Baghel Singh this time advised them to hand it over to the *Mahant* who would take care of the newly built Gurdwara. The *chola* was handed over to the *Mahant* of the shrine. In the course of time, it got lost.

Socio-cultural activities

The daily activities and religious rituals of the Gurdwara Rakab Ganj Sahib start with *Prakash* at 3.30 a.m. The daily programmes include recitations of *Sukhmani Sahib, Panch Bani of Nitnem, Japji, Asa-di-Var, Guru Itihaas Katha, Rehras, Gurbani, Sohila,* and singing of *Kirtan* followed by *Ardas, Hukamnama* and *Prasad. Akhand Path* is also undertaken every day in the special room where the *Guru Granth Sahib* is rested on a *Manji Sahib*.

Gurdwara Rakab Ganj Sahib celebrates most of the *Gurpurb*s specially the birth anniversaries of Guru Nanak, Guru Tegh Bahadur and Guru Gobind Singh, and the martyrdom anniversary of Guru Tegh Bahadur. A procession is organized every year by the Guru's devotees to commemorate his martyrdom. The procession follows the same route and by-lanes which Lakhi Shah had followed for carrying Guru Tegh Bahadur's body from Chandi Chowk to where Gurdwara Rakab Ganj is now located, through Nai Sarak, Chawri Bazar, Ajmeri Gate, Pahar Ganj, Panchkuyian Road and Connaught Place. Big *Dewan*s are also held here on *Gurpurb*s.

Apart from the *Guru-ka-Langar*, '*Sabad-ka-Langar*' is also offered to all who come to the Gurdwara for participation in worship and prayer, through traditionally established practices such as organized *Kirtan* and *Katha*.

The number of visitors and devotees to this Gurdwara is comparatively less than the other historical Gurdwaras in Delhi. Even the attendence in the community kitchen is very thin, specially during week days. However, on Sundays, on the occasion of *Gurpurb*s and other specific days when some Sikh rites and ceremonies are performed in the Gurdwara premises, the number of visitors increase. Since the Gurdwara is located in the same complex as the office of the Delhi Sikh Gurdwara Management Committee, rallies and special programmes on the occasion of *Gurpurb*s are held here throughout the year. During these occasions, the influx of visitors and devotees into this Gurdwara complex, sometimes become unperceivable.

Other relevant information

Gurdwara Rakab Ganj Sahib and its complex is stretched over 14 acres of land in a prime location of the capital city. Besides the main Gurdwara building, the complex houses the *Guru-ka-Langar* hall (in two parts) and *Gurmat Vidyalaya* (Teaching Centre for learning of the tenets of Sikh faith and Sikh theology); Gurupdesh Printing Press where most of the publications on Sikh history and religion including printing of the *Guru Granth Sahib* are undertaken; staff quarters (57 flats); offices of Akali Dal; *Sarai* for the V.I.P.s; Lakhi Shah Vanjara hall where marriages, *Gurpurb*s, etc. are held, and lastly, the office of the Delhi Sikh Gurdwara Management Committee and a newly built office complex in its annexe.

The 80 feet deep well, 12 feet in diameter (approximately), that still exists right behind the *Karah Prasad* collection centre of the Gurdwara complex deserves a special mention in this context. It is believed that the water of this well was used by Lakhi Shah's family for bathing the headless body of Guru Tegh Bahadur before his cremation. With the water level having gone down, the well at present is dry.

Moti Bagh Sahib

ਦੇਗ ਤੇਗ ਫਤਹਿ
ਨਾਸਰੋ ਮਨਸੂਰ ਗੁਰੁ ਗੋਬਿੰਦ ਸਿੰਘ।
ਏਜ਼ਦੀ ਮਨਜ਼ੂਰ ਗੁਰੁ ਗੋਬਿੰਦ ਸਿੰਘ।।

Historical background and associated myths and legends

Gurdwara Moti Bagh Sahib situated on the Ring road near the Moti Bagh Colony, is considered as one of the important sacred places by the Sikhs, as the place was sanctified by the visit of the last Sikh Guru, Guru Gobind Singh. While paying a visit to this Gurdwara, the visitors and devotees pay homage to their great religious leader who, according to Historian Mohmmad Latiff, "Was a lawgiver in the pulpit, a champion in the field, a king on his Masand and a Faquir in the society of Khalsa"(54). Guru Gobind Singh was not only a 'mere ideal' for the Punjabi community, but humanity as a whole. He stood for secularism, national unity, and emotional integration of the Indian people. "The Guru created the Khalsa, transferred sovereignty to the poor and oppressed of our country, so that they might remember in the days to come that there was in history, too, a Guru by the name Gobind Singh who taught ideals of democracy, secularism, brotherhood and unity of mankind" (S.S.Johar, *Hand Book on Sikhism*). The people still regard him as one of the greatest Indians of all ages.

Guru Gobind Singh, the Tenth Guru of the Sikhs (1666-1708 C.E.), who visited Delhi and camped at the place where Gurdwara Moti Bagh Sahib is located.

After the death of the Mughal Emperor Aurangzeb in February, 1707 C.E., Prince Muazzam (later known as Bahadur Shah), was in Afghanistan on an expedition. Prince Azam, younger brother of Prince Muazzam, took advantage of the situation. He declared himself the Emperor and assumed command of the Imperial Army. Prince Muazzam lost no time in reaching Delhi, but found Prince Azam to be stronger than him. Before jumping into the fray, Prince Muazzam thought of Guru Gobind Singh of whom he had heard a lot. He appealed to Guru Gobind Singh for help in the battle of succession between him and his younger brother Prince Azam. The Guru promised to help but on the condition that when Prince Muazzam came to power, he would punish those responsible for killing his sons treacherously and uprooting him from his city, Anandpur. Prince Muazzam agreed in principle and a meeting between him and the Guru was fixed at Delhi in the last week of May, 1707 C.E.

As scheduled, Guru Gobind Singh reached Delhi with his *Khalsa* army and camped at the place called Mochi Bagh (now known as Moti Bagh), the colony of tanners owned by a rich *Baniya* named Moti Ram.

While staying in a camp at Moti Bagh, the Guru shot an arrow into the Red Fort to inform Prince Muazzam of his arrival. It is said that the shooting of the arrow was so accurate that it straight away struck the high and spacious cot of the Prince camping at the Red Fort. The Prince took this for a miracle, but when a second arrow came from Guru Gobind Singh, it carried a note saying that it was not a miracle, but a sheer skill in archery. The Prince was impressed with Guru Gobind Singh's skill in archery and acknowledged his supremacy. "From Guru Gobind Singh's own accounts as to the way he used his weapons in his wars, we learn that the Guru was a superb archer able to shoot three to four arrows in a single shot, and he could shoot arrows with both hands with equal dexterity"(55).

The meeting between Prince Muazzam and the Guru was proposed to be held at the place near Humayun's Tomb, where Gurdwara Damdama Sahib stands now.

Page 104: *A close view of the Tirsthan built on a solid stone wall with Nishan Sahib. From this spot Guru Gobind Singh shot two arrows into the Red Fort to inform Prince Muazzam (later known as Bahadur Shah) of his arrival in Delhi.*

Pages 102-103: *A night view of Gurdwara Moti Bagh located on the Ring Road near Moti Bagh Government Colony. This is the place where Guru Gobind Singh camped with his Khalsa Army.*

Architectural details: An overview

At the place where Guru Gobind Singh camped and from where the Guru shot two arrows into the Red Fort to inform Prince Muazzam of his arrival, now stands Gurdwara Moti Bagh.

According to what the old local residents of the village Mochi Bagh (Moti Bagh) have to report, it may be assumed that the original entrance to the present Gurdwara complex was from the southern side, where an old well (measuring about 20 feet in circumference and made of heavy stones) still exists. The people of the erstwhile village of Mochi Bagh used to move through this entrance. The old well, which is not used by the villagers any more, may have once been the regular source of drinking water not only for the villagers, but also for Guru Gobind Singh when he camped here. The place from where the Guru shot two arrows (known as *Tirsthan*) into the Red Fort was a high, solid stone wall with a *Nishan Sahib* originally fixed by Guru Gobind Singh. Moving further through the old main entrance, there was an open shed on a high spacious platform (locally known as *Chubara*) where the Guru used to meet visitors during his stay at Mochi Bagh.

As the old main entrance from the southern side of the Gurdwara complex is now replaced with a thick boundary wall, and the new

The old well (measuring about 20 feet in circumference and made of heavy stones) is now seen to be covered with debris. The well is located outside the southern boundary wall of the Moti Bagh Gurdwara complex.

Gurdwara building stands on the site of the old *Chubara*, no one can find anything of the past except relying on the verbal statements of the old local residents of Mochi Bagh (Moti Bagh). Even the *Tirsthan*, from where Guru Gobind Singh shot arrows, is covered with white marble and lot of changes have been made at the time of the construction of a new Gurdwara complex in 1980-81. The place where Guru Gobind Singh used to recite *Japji* early in the morning is now converted into a room accessible by a separate entrance along the southern boundary wall. This room is used as the resting room for the *Guru Granth Sahib*. The *Tirsthan*, which is now converted into a three-story complex facing the main Gurdwara building also has two rooms in the first floor and three rooms in the ground floor. All these rooms are used for non-stop reading (*Akhand Path*) of the text of the *Guru Granth Sahib*. The present Gurdwara building has a flat roof with a high gateway on the east. It has been constructed by Late Baba Harbans Singh in 1980-81. Built on a raised plinth, the building is a beautified compact structure with rich architectural decorations. It has several domes, some big and some small. The inside walls of the building are decorated with inlaid designs

A showcase bedecked with a variety of weapons is located just near the Sukhasan room.

and motifs, as also found in other reconstructed historical Gurdwaras of Delhi. The Gurdwara has twelve doors on four sides, the *Prakash Asthan*, the *Sukhasan* room and also underground parking space just near the main entrance.

Socio-cultural activities

Gurdwara Moti Bagh Sahib celebrates birthdays of Guru Nanak and Guru Gobind Singh, but the installation anniversary of the *Guru Granth Sahib* celebrated on August 17 every year is considered to be of greatest significance. Some scholars are also invited to give discourse on various aspects of the *Guru Granth Sahib*. *Guru-ka-Langar* plays an important role in promoting social harmony among the people of the nearby areas. Special *Guru-ka-Langar*s arranged on Fridays and Sundays attract about 1,000-1,200 visitors, the majority being Hindus. *Guru-ka-Langar* is not an act of pity or charity. It is based on the concept of, "*Dana Pani Guruka, Tahil Seva Sikhan Ki*", which means, "the provisions are from the Guru, only service and love belong to the Sikhs, the servants of *Sangat*, God and the Guru."

The Sukhasan room located in the north-west corner of the main hall of the Gurdwara building in which the Guru Granth Sahib is rested during the night.

Damdama Sahib

ਸ਼ਾਹ ਦਰਵੇਸ਼ ਗੁਰ ਗੋਬਿੰਦ ਸਿੰਘ

Historical background and associated myths and legends

Located behind Humayun's tomb and just opposite Nizamuddin Railway Station, Gurdwara Damdama Sahib marks the spot where Guru Gobind Singh first met Prince Muazzam, later known as Emperor Bahadur Shah. Prince Muazzam was aware of how the Guru fought a fierce battle against the Mughal forces at Nadaun (about 30 kilometres from Kangra, Himachal Pradesh) in 1690 C.E. The Guru fought this battle to protect the rulers of Kangra and Bilaspur when they were attacked by the Mughal Imperial Army for not paying tribute to the Mughal Emperor Aurangzeb.

When Guru Gobind Singh came to Delhi on Prince Muazzam's invitation, the Guru and Prince Muazzam discussed war plans and the strategy for the final battle of succession.

As planned, Prince Muazzam and Guru Gobind Singh sent their forces to capture Agra, which was under the forcible occupation of Prince Azam. The two armies met at Jajau on June 8, 1707 C.E. According to Punjabi historical document *Bahadur Shah ke Mulakat ka Prasang*, Guru Gobind Singh first sent his regiment commander with an army unit under Bhai Dharam Singh. What ensued was a stormy fight that reached a critical phase. Bidar Bakht, the brave son of Azam was killed, and then Azam himself was also killed in the battlefield. Ten thousand men died in this battle. "After the victory, Prince Muazzam expressed his gratitude to Guru Gobind Singh in many ways and also offered Khillat

Facing page: *A view of the Prakash Asthan located inside the Damdama Sahib Gurdwara building.*

Pages 110-111: *A close view of Gurdwara Damdama Sahib located behind Humayun's tomb and just opposite Nizamuddin Railway Station, New Delhi. This Gurdwara marks the spot where Guru Gobind Singh first met Prince Muazzam.*

to Guruji. The Prince was then declared the new Mughal Emperor of Delhi"(56).

Architectural details: An overview

The Gurdwara constructed by Late Baba Harbans Singh with the help of the Sikh *Sangat*s, stands on a high walled compound entered through a gateway with a pointed arch. The main building of the Gurdwara is a compact two-storeyed structure with high ceilinged walls, and with a gallery running along its walls at mid-height. It has a square *Prakash Asthan* and a resting room for the *Guru Granth Sahib*. The Gurdwara building is covered with white marble and the interiors are decorated with floral designs and motifs composed of cut glass pieces of white, green, blue and pink colours. The Gurdwara facing west has twelve doors on four sides, which also display beautifully carved designs on marble. It is reported that all the decorative designs were executed mainly by Muslim artisans from Rajasthan. As in other Gurdwaras, this Gurdwara also has a room for *Akhand Path*.

The ground floor of the Gurdwara has a spacious hall which is used for accommodating tourists and pilgrims, especially during the summer season when they halt here overnight, on their way to Kedarnath, Badrinath and Hemkunt Sahib in Uttarakhand.

Daily programmes

The Gurdwara performs certain daily programmes which start early morning and continues upto 8.30 p.m. The daily programmes include *Guru Granth Sahibji-ka-Prakash, Sukhmani-Sahibji-ka-Path,* recitation of *Nitnem, Ardas, Hukam,* recitation of *Asa-di-Var,* distribution of *Karah-prasad,* reading of *Sodar* and *Sohila,* singing of scriptural hymns, *Kirtan* and lastly, *Sukhasan* which marks the end of the day's programme.

In the Gurdwara, devotees sit on the floor irrespective of their status in society. No distinction is made between Sikh or non Sikh devotees. No special favours are extended to any individual or person.

Facing Page: *A full view of the Gurdwara Damdama Sahib.*

ਸਤਿਨਾਮੁ ਵਾਹਿਗੁਰੂ
ਜਉ ਤਉ ਪ੍ਰੇਮ ਖੇਲਨ ਕਾ ਚਾਉ ਸਿਰ ਧਰ ਤਲੀ ਗਲੀ ਮੇਰੀ ਆਉ

It deserves a special mention in this context that in the Sikh shrines, women and men enjoy an equal status. Women can go to the congregations without any restrictions, they have equal rights of worship and baptism, they can participate in all the religious ceremonies, and can lead the service in the Gurdwara as well as in the community kitchen. Naturally, a common man in the Sikh society tends to believe in womens' equality in society. The credit for this goes to Guru Nanak and the successive Gurus. Guru Nanak declared that, "Women must be respected because they are the source of man's physical existence and the entire social life. Man is attached to the world through them"(57).

Gurdwara Damdama Sahib has a spacious community kitchen where cooked food is served to all visitors. Approximately, 200-300 visitors share meals here everyday. On Sundays, however, the number of visitors is reported to be more than 500 as special food is served. An on-the-spot study reveals that most of the visitors come from the nearby localities and belong to not only the Sikh, but also the Hindu, and the Muslim communities. The institution of *Guru-ka-Langar* introduced by the Sikh Gurus bear testimony to the fact that religious instructions sound hollow and hypocritical to a hungry man.

Guru-ka-Langar at Gurdwara Damdama Sahib where special food is served on Sundays.

Socio-cultural activities

The rites and ceremonies performed at the Gurdwara mainly include birth ceremony, naming ceremony, marriage ceremony and death ceremony. No ceremony is complete without offering *Arda*s. One of the special cultural programmes celebrated with great enthusiasm in this Gurdwara is the festival of *Hola Mohalla,* the festival of the spring season in the month of March (next day of *Holi*). Apart from *Kirtan Darbar,* a *Mela* is arranged in the Gurdwara complex in which people from various localities display their merchandise. The *Mela* is visited by thousands of visitors and devotees.

Gurdwara Damdama Sahib has a special role to play in the months of May and June every year when 500-1,000 *Yatrie*s (pilgrims including foreigners), drop-in here from Nizamuddin Railway Station on their way to Hemkunt Sahib in Uttarakhand where Guru Gobind Singh is believed to have meditated for a very long time in his previous incarnation. Most of the pilgrims come from different states of India and stay here for a few hours for taking rest before they resume their onward journey to Hemkunt Sahib. Gurdwara Damdama (literally meaning temporay resting place) Sahib provides food and shelter in its large hall, which also serves as an additional place of accommodation for the pilgrims.

Other relevant information

Old local residents of the area still remember the existence of an old neem tree and a well in the area which now forms a part of the boundary of the Gurdwara complex. Sardar Chandan Singh, a close associate of Master Tara Singh (who was one of the foremost political leaders of the erstwhile *Akali Dal,* Punjab), confidently reports that the old neem tree was used as a medicinal plant by the local residents. The old well was used as a source of drinking water by the local residents. The old neem tree was uprooted and the old well was filled with soil and permanently closed at the time when construction of the new Gurdwara building was undertaken by Late Baba Harbans Singh.

Mata Sundari

ਤੀਰ ਤੁਹੀ ਸੈਥੀ ਤੁਹੀ ਤੁਹੀ ਤਬਰ ਤਰਵਾਰ ਨਾਮ ਤਿਹਾਰੋ ਜੋ ਜਪੈ, ਭਏ ਸਿੰਧ ਭਵ
ਜ. ਬਾਬਾ ਹਰਬੰਸ ਸਿੰਘ ਜੀ ਗੁ.
ਬੰਗਲਾ ਸਾਹਿਬ ਦਿੱਲੀ. ਕਾਰ ਸੇਵਾ
ਲਈ ਮਾਇਆ ਗੋਲਕ ਵਿਚ ਪਾਓ ਜੀ

Historical background and associated myths and legends

Gurdwara Mata Sundari was originally known as 'Mata Sundari ki Haveli' and later transformed into a Gurdwara by Sardar Baghel Singh in 1783 C.E., in memory of Mata Sundari and Mata Sahib Kaur, the two illustrious wives of Guru Gobind Singh. They took great interest in politics and guided the destiny of the Sikhs after the death of the Guru on October 7, 1708 C.E. This Gurdwara can be classified as a historical Gurdwara but not a historical shrine as Guru Gobind Singh did not visit this place. This Gurdwara may be classified as historical because this is the place where Mata Sundari and Mata Sahib Kaur lived for a long time, and from where they led and served the *Khalsa Panth* and resolved the dispute between the *Bandai*s (the followers of Banda Bahadur) and the *Tat Khalsa* (the main body of the Sikhs) in the year 1721 C.E.

After the victory in the war of succession, Prince Muazzam ascended the throne as Emperor Bahadur Shah. In September 1708 C.E., Bahadur Shah invited Guru Gobind Singh to meet him at Agra. Guru Gobind Singh met the Emperor at Agra. The latter not only received the Guru with due respect and costly presents, but also invited him to accompany him (the Emperor) in his expedition to quell the rebellion of his brother in the south. The Emperor was, however, tactfully avoiding the question of punishing those who were responsible for bricking alive the Guru's two younger sons (Zorawar Singh and Fateh Singh) on December 27, 1704 C.E.

Facing page: *Prakash Asthan inside the building of the Gurdwara Mata Sundari.*

Pages 118-119: *A general view of Gurdwara Mata Sundari located at Mata Sundari lane, New Delhi. Here the two illustrious wives of Guru Gobind Singh, named Mother Sundari and Mother Sahib Kaur, lived in a haveli known as Mata Sundari ki Haveli which was later transformed into a Gurdwara.*

at Sirhind under the orders of its Viceroy, Wazir Khan. Nonetheless, the Guru agreed to travel with him as he had an intention to camp at Nanded (formerly in Hyderabad state and now in Maharashtra).

When the Guru was about to leave Delhi for Nanded, Mata Sahib Kaur, who had taken a vow not to touch her meals until she had a *Darshan* of the Guru each day, insisted on her going with him. The Guru acceded to her appeal reluctantly but after sometime, Guru Gobind Singh persuaded his wife Mata Sahib Kaur to return to Delhi and join his other wife Mata Sundari. Mata Sahib Kaur was unwilling to return from Nanded leaving the Guru behind. The Guru explained to her that whenever she desired to see him, she could just have a glimpse of his weapons that he had gifted her at Delhi. Convinced, Mata Sahib Kaur, accompanied by Bhai Mani Singh, a devotee of the Guru and his scribe, returned to Delhi. Thereafter, Mata Sahib Kaur would always have a *Darshan* of these weapons before her meals.

Both Mata Sundari and Mata Sahib Kaur came to Delhi at a critical phase of their lives when Guru Gobind Singh, in his battle against the tyranny of the Mughal army, (under Emperor Aurangzeb) lost five members of his family including his old mother. Two of his sons, Ajit Singh and Jujhar Singh, sacrificed their lives in the battle of Chamkaur Sahib (district Ropar, Punjab) on December 22, 1704 C.E., while his other two younger sons, "Zorawar Singh and Fateh Singh were bricked alive in Sirhind on December 27, 1704 C.E."(58). After his escape from Chamkaur, Guru Gobind Singh was tarvelling around in disguise. He first came to Machhiwara (an old town of Ludhiana district, Punjab) and then reached Raikot (also in Ludhiana district). When the Guru heard the shocking news at Raikot he said:

Mortal is this frame unenduring and perishable,
Praise of the Divine is the raft by which is this worldly ocean securely crossed.

On hearing this devastating news, Mata Gujari, the Guru's mother, collapsed on the spot and died. Agonized by the cruel death of his younger sons, and his old mother, Guru Gobind Singh left Raikot for Malwa tract of the Punjab in disguise. Bhai Mani Singh escorted the Guru's two wives, Mata Sundari and Mata Sahib Kaur to Delhi. Since then they had been residing at the Kucha Dilwali Singhan Haveli near Ajmeri gate. During their stay here until 1725 C.E., they were attended by Kirpal Chand (maternal uncle of Guru Gobind Singh), and Sahib Singh, brother of Mata Sahib Kaur. When the holy mothers parted from Guru Gobind Singh, Mata Sundari sought the Guru's permission to adopt as her son, a boy who looked exactly like her eldest son Ajit Singh. Guru Gobind Singh agreed with reluctance, warning her that the adopted boy's physical resemblance to their own son Ajit Singh could in no way ensure the similarity in their character. The adopted son was named Ajit Singh.

Mata Sahib Kaur was made the eternal mother of the *Khalsa*. She was given five weapons: one Sword, one *Khanda* (double edged sword), one *Khanjar* (poniard) and two *Katar*s (daggers), also known as *Jamdhars*, out of which three are now missing. Mata Sahib Kaur was also authorized to use the Guru's seal-symbol on the *Hukamnama*s. Dr. Trilochan Singh, on the basis of the letters of both the holy mothers in his possession, confirms that, "Only Mata Sahib Kaur's letters bear this seal-symbol (a sort of cross)" (59).

In the absence of Guru Gobind Singh, the last Guru (tenth in succession), Ajit Singh, the adopted son of Mata Sundari, planned to become the eleventh Guru of the Sikhs. Unable to tolerate his high-handedness and audacity, Mata Sundari disowned him. Soon after this, the ill-fated adopted son was rightly or wrongly implicated in the murder of a Muslim *Fakir*, and was killed by being tied to the

Facing Page Top: *A painting showing Guru Gobind Singh's two younger sons namely, Zorawar Singh and Fateh Singh facing trial before Nawab Wazir Khan. They were asked to accept Islam but they refused to renounce their religion.*

Facing Page Bottom: *As ordered by Nawab Wazir Khan, Zorawar Singh and Fateh Singh were bricked alive in Sirhind on December, 27, 1704 C.E.*

tail of an elephant and dragged through the city on June 18, 1725 C.E. Subsequent to the execution of Ajit Singh, Mata Sundari and Mata Sahib Kaur thought it safer to move out of Delhi. They left for Mathura and stayed there for two years, and came back to Delhi when the matter subsided. The Maharaja of Jaipur had arranged for their stay at Mathura. When both the mothers came back from Mathura, they made their abode in a house outside Turkman Gate about two kilometers south of Chandni Chowk. This house popularly called Mata Sundari Ki Haveli afterwards came to be known as Gurdwara Mata Sundari.

During his stay at Nanded (September-October 1708 C.E.), Guru Gobind Singh used to address various congregations. One day, while the Guru was addressing a big congregation, a young and well built Pathan named Jasmid Khan, came and bowed his head in reverence. The Guru showed him due courtesy and gave him a place of honour in his *Darbar*. The Pathan used to visit the Guru's *Darbar* regularly and nobody, including the Guru, was ever suspicious about the real intentions of the Pathan. In reality, he was sent by Wazir Khan, the *Faujdar* of Sirhind to kill the Guru. On Septemer 20, 1708 C.E., the Pathan came again to visit the Guru's *Darbar* and remained there for a much longer time than usual. After the congregation was over, the Guru went to his tent. The Pathan followed him and bowed before the Guru. When the Guru raised his head to bless him, the Pathan took out his dagger and struck the Guru with it. Though Guru Gobind Singh did kill him with his *Kirpan* on the spot, the Guru had seriously wounded himself and bled profusely. The Guru's wounds were bandaged and later, Emperor Bahadur Shah's European surgeon Cole, stitched the Guru's wounds with great skill. The Guru was completely healed in about fifteen days but one day while trying to bend a beautiful bow presented to him by one of his devotees, his wound got unstiched, and he started to bleed profusely. On October 7, 1708 C.E., the Guru left his earthly abode at Nanded. At the sight where the Guru breathed his last, a Gurdwara called Takht Sachkhand Sri Hazur Sahib Abichal Nagar was built.

After the death of Guru Gobind Singh at Nanded, Mata Sundari, took great interest in political affairs and guided the destiny of the Sikhs. The Sikhs used to gather in her *haveli*. She was held in high esteem by all and her instructions were obeyed. It is from this *haveli* that Mata Sundari resolved the dispute between the *Banda*is (the followers of Banda Bahadur, a great devotee of Guru Gobind Singh who was baptized by the Guru during his stay at Nanded), and the *Tat Khalsa* (the main body of the Sikhs), in the year 1721 C.E. She deputed her late husband's scribe Bhai Mani Singh, the most respected Sikh of the time, to go to Amritsar and sort out the differences and to mediate between the two groups so that the matter was settled once and for all. Later, when the dispute was resolved Mata Sundari asked Bhai Mani Singh to take over the charge of administering the *Harimandir*. It is known from available sources that Bhai Shihan Singh, another scribe, received the sacred writings of Guru Gobind Singh from Bhai Mani Singh at the *haveli* of Mata Sundari, and revised those writings. It is also said that Guru Gobind Singh might have dictated some portions of the *Guru Granth Sahib* to Bhai Mani Singh at Damdama Sahib before he left for Nanded in September, 1708 C.E.

Mata Sundari died in this sacred *haveli* in *Samvat* 1804 *Vikrami* (1747 C.E.). The exact date of Mata Sahib Kaur's death is not known, but it is believed that she passed away some time before Mata Sundari's death in 1747 C.E.

The *Samadhi*s of both the holy mothers exist today in the compound of Gurdwara Bala Sahib built by Sardar Baghel Singh.

After the death of Mata Sahib Kaur, the weapons that Guru Gobind Singh had gifted her were preserved by Bhai Jiwan Singh (a trusted person of Guru Gobind Singh's family) and later by his descendents in their house in the Chitli Kabar Mohalla of Matya Bazar, somewhere near Turkman Gate, old Delhi. "The place became

sanctified by the presence of these weapons. The weapons were later shifted to Gurdwara Rakab Ganj"(60).

Architectural details: An overview

Gurdwara Mata Sundari situated at Mata Sundari lane, New Delhi, has a palatial and impressive three-storey building today, which has come up in the recent years through *Karseva* supervised by Late Baba Harbans Singh.

The Gurdwara building facing north has four doors on four sides, but it has seventeen windows which gives the visitor an impression that the building has been designed keeping the *haveli* style in mind, similar to Mata Sundari's original residence for about 40 years. The flat roof of the building is supported by six main pillars which is not usually seen in other historical Gurdwaras in Delhi. The central dome of the building rests on a separate room constructed over the roof. The facade of the building has bay windows on the first floor and decorative domed kiosks on the roof-top.

Socio-cultural activities

As Gurdwara Mata Sundari was not sanctified by the sacred visit of any of the Gurus, the number of visitors and devotees appear to be much thinner here as compared to other historical Gurdwaras of Delhi. Even on Sundays, the *Guru-ka-Langar* receives only a few visitors. The daily programmes including congregational prayers and such are less in number. The only special function organized here on a large scale on December 27 every year is the death anniversary of Guru Gobind Singh's sons.

It is significant to remember in this connection that it was during the month of December (December 21-22) in the year 1704 C.E., that Guru Gobind Singh lost two of his elder sons, Ajit Singh and Jujhar Singh in a fierce historical battle at Chamkaur against the mighty Mughal army. At Chamkaur, a new chapter of bravery, valour and heroism of Guru

Facing Page: *A side view of Gurdwara Mata Sundari showing fourteen windows and a plain boundary wall.*

Gobind Singh's sons was added in the history of mankind. Chamkaur is considered a sacred place sanctified by the blood of the Guru's two elder sons. Magnificent Gurdwaras stand here today in memory of the great events that had created history. To commemorate the great events and specially the glorious deaths of Guru Gobind Singh's sons, Mata Sundari Gurdwara arranges a special annual fair on December 27 every year in a manner similar to that arranged at Chamkaur Sahib on December 21 and 22.

Other relevant information

Apart from the Gurdwara's regular activities, the following must find a mention.

Gurbani Sangeet Academy: Run under the auspices of the Delhi Sikh Gurdwara Management Committee, the academy teaches *Kirtan* and *Tabla* playing.

Gurmat College: The college related to the Punjabi University, Patiala, offers under-graduate and post-graduate courses both in English and Punjabi for *Gurmat* studies and basic tenets of Sikhism. The college also offers courses like B.A. and M.A. in Sikh studies, M.A. in Religious studies and M.A. in *Gurmat Sangeet*. The college also offers courses like Diploma in Divinity, Diploma in *Gurmat Sangeet* and *Gyani*. A short-term study course on the *Guru Granth Sahib* has also been introduced recently.

The teachings of *Gurmat* not only play an important role in the socio-cultural life of the Sikhs, but also contribute towards the transmission of the messege of self-reliance among all classes of people in the society. Right from Guru Nanak, Sikhism tried to inspire and carry with it the whole Indian nation. The Sikh Gurus declared that the whole human race was one, and, that an individual was to be respected not because he or she belonged to any particular class or creed, but because God created them. Sikhism believes that since all human beings received their souls from God, they should all be treated alike.

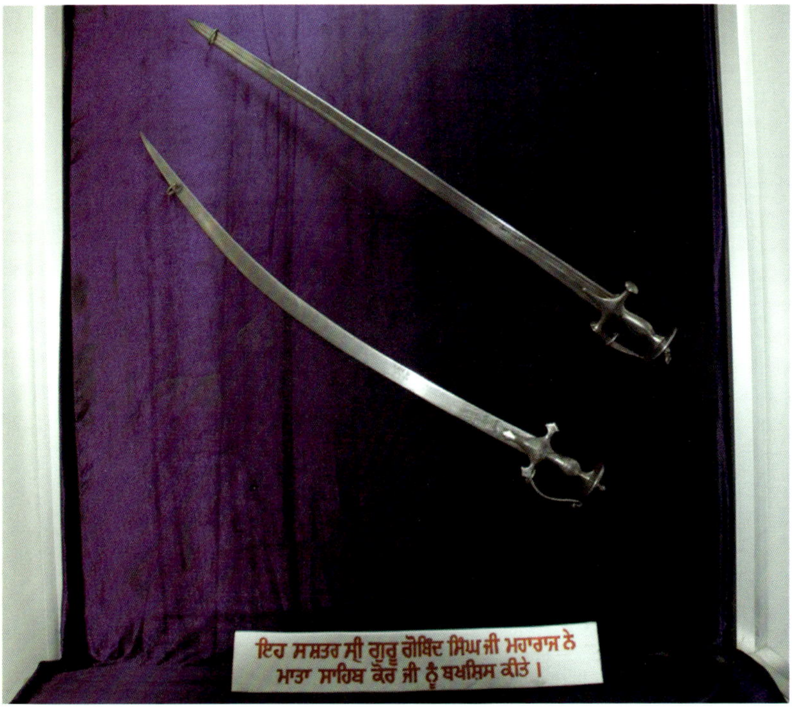

These two swords kept in the Mata Sundari Gurdwara were given as gifts to Mata Sahib Kaur by Guru Gobind Singh.

The tenets of Sikhism were basically concerned with the development of human beings, their own ethics and moral character. Guru Gobind Singh, who proclaimed that all men were equal, and that only outer forms differed, said in *Akal Ustat, 86*:

Recognize all humans as one,
All men are the same,
Although they appear different under different influences.
The bright and the dark, the ugly and the beautiful,
The Hindus and the Muslims, have developed themselves
according to the fashions of different countries.
All have the same eyes, the same ears, the same body
and the same build—a compound of the same four elements (61).

Baba Banda Singh Bahadur

Historical background and associated myths and legends

Gurdwara Baba Banda Singh Bahadur located at Mehrauli, New Delhi, was built to commemorate the martyrdom of Banda Bahadur and the death of his four year old son and many other Sikhs at this place in 1716 C.E. It is not a Sikh shrine, but certainly a historical Gurdwara as it unveils Banda Singh Bahadur's supreme sacrifice for the sake of his countrymen. His continuous fight against the oppressive Mughal Empire made him a great national hero. Though Banda Bahadur was a demon in the eyes of the Muslims, he was considered to be the first empire builder for the Sikhs. As a devout follower of Guru Gobind Singh, he imbibed in him the high ideals of sincerity, honesty, indomitable spirit, unbounded enthusiasm, rare daring, and single-minded devotion to his cause. Mohammad Latif, a noted historian, however, says, "That Guru Gobind Singh had selected Banda for avenging the death of his father and two sons, for which purpose he could not have singled out a better instrument than this ruthless blood-sucker"(62).

Banda Singh Bahadur aroused the spirit of the Sikhs against the oppressive Mughal rule in Punjab, and his unshaken faith in Sikhism had been the cause of his martyrdom.

Guru Gobind Singh died on October 7, 1708 C.E., at Nanded. Just before his death, the Guru appointed a hermit from Poonch (Jammu and Kashmir) then settled in Nanded, named Banda Singh Bahadur,

Facing page: *A side view of the Gurdwara Banda Singh Bahadur at Mehrauli.*

Pages 130-131: *A view of Gurdwara Banda Singh Bahadur located near Khwaja Qutab-Ud-Din Bakhtiyar Kaki Dargah (near Qutab Minar, Meharuli). The building is smaller in size; it has only one large-sized dome on the top.*

as the leader of the Sikh *Panth*. He was baptized by the Guru. Banda received *Pahul* and became a Sikh. The Guru specifically directed Banda to protect the people from the onslaught of Wazir Khan. The Guru gave him a *Hukamnama*, addressed to the Sikhs all over the country, in which the Sikhs were called upon to gather under Banda's banner and obey his commands. During his northward journey from the Deccan, Banda came to know that Guru Gobind Singh had been stabbed by an assassin sent by Wazir Khan.

Determined to punish this tyrant and his Hindu accomplice Suchanand, Banda marched with his swelling army towards Sirhind in October, 1708 C.E. His main objective was to establish a Sikh state, obtain national independence, and avenge the heinous crime of the murder of Guru Gobind Singh and his two younger sons. On his way to Sirhind, Banda mobilized the downtrodden peasants who he liberated from slavery of the feudal lords and made them complete owners and masters of the land they tilled. These peasants joined him in countless numbers. Sirhind was sacked. Wazir Khan and Suchanand were killed. The whole of the province of Sirhind was occupied. Coins were struck and the sovereignty of the *Khalsa* was established over nearly the whole of Punjab including the east of Lahore upto Jammu hills. The Hindu Chiefs of the Sivalik hills who constantly caused trouble to Guru Gobind Singh and helped the Mughal armies in the destruction of Anandpur were also chastised. After establishing his sway in Punjab, Banda shifted his capital from Sirhind to Mukhlispur, a hilly place near Sadhura (district Sirmaur, Himachal Pradesh), built a fortress there and called it Lohgarh (fort of iron). The hill Rajas apprehending attack from Banda, surrendered.

After the death of Bahadur Shah on February 18, 1712 C.E., Farrukhsiyar became the Emperor after dethroning the son of

A view of the Prakash Asthan of the Gurdwara Banda Singh Bahadur.

Facing Page: *The obverse and reverse of a coin issued by Sardar Banda Singh Bahadur.*

Bahadur Shah in 1713 C.E. He instructed Zakariya Khan, the Punjab Governor to kill Banda at any cost and completely annihilate the Sikhs. For nearly five years, Banda and his men continued to remain a terror for their enemies, till at last, the Mughal army helped by the Hindu Chiefs of the hill states, seized Banda's army at Gurdas Nangal, near

Gurdaspur, Punjab. "Banda and his men surrendered after eight months of fighting and that was because months of starvation had made them utterly weak and helpless. On December 7, 1715 C.E., Banda was arrested" (63).

Heavily chained and locked in an iron cage, Banda was brought to Delhi on February 29, 1716 C.E. All prisoners including Banda were offered the usual choice of choosing death or adopting Islam, but all chose death. The execution of Banda and his companions began on March 3, 1716 C.E., under the supervision of Kotwal Sarbarah Khan, opposite the Police Station in old Delhi. According to historian Muhammad Latif, Banda and his fellow prisoners were made to suffer untold indignities. They were made to wear sheep's skin, and, seated on donkeys and camels, and were paraded through the crowded streets of Delhi.

This happened on March 10, 1716 C.E. Banda was heading this procession of the Sikh captives. Banda's face was blackened, and he was forced to sit in an iron cage, placed upon an elephant and dressed, out of mockery, in a gold embroidered red turban and a heavy robe of bright-red colour brocade embroidered with pomegranate flowers in gold. Behind him stood an executioner with a naked sword in his hand. "The road from Agharabad to the Lahori gate of the city, a distance of several miles, was lined on both sides with troops, and filled with exultant crowds, who mocked at Banda Singh and laughed at the grotesque appearance of his followers"(64). Everyday, a hundred brave men perished, and at night the headless bodies were loaded into carts, taken out of the city and hung on trees. It was June 9, 1716 C.E., and Banda still had not agreed to adopting Islam as his religion, and when all efforts failed to buy him off, Banda was taken through the streets of the city to the shrine of Sufi Saint Khwaja Bakhtiyar Kaki, near the Qutab Minar, and paraded around the tomb of Emperor Bahadur Shah. Once again, he was offered a choice—adopt Islam or choose death. Banda chose death.

On the day of Banda's execution, his four year old son Ajay Singh was put in his clasp and Banda was asked to kill him. He refused. On refusal, the innocent child was brutally killed, and his heart was taken out and thrust into the mouth of his father, Banda Singh.

According to Khafi Khan, the author of *Muntakhib-ul-Lubab*, Mohammad Amin Khan, one of the tribunal members, struck by Banda's extraordinary appearance, and impressed by the acuteness in his countenance and nobility in his conduct asked Banda, "How a man with such noble and virtuous bearing could be guilty of such horrors?" Banda replied in a calm and stoic voice, "In every faith and every land whenever men become corrupt, despotic and tyrannous, then the Divine Avenger never fails to raise up a scourge like me to punish them and teach them a lesson. And for all the excesses a man like me had to commit, to punish the evil doers, God deemed it fit to make me atone for them in this life only through sufferings".

A painting showing Banda Singh Bahadur seeking blessings and advice from Guru Gobind Singh on the eve of his departure from Nanded to Punjab alongwith five Sikhs.

After this Banda was tortured to death in front of the *Kotwali* yard. His eyes were removed with a knife. His left foot was cut off. His flesh was torn from his body with red hot pincers and then his body was cut to pieces limb by limb. "Resigned to the will of God, he died on Sunday, June 9, 1716 C.E., unshaken in his faith in Sikhism," says historian Mountstaurt Elphinstone, in his book titled *An Account of the Kingdom of Cabul.* He says, "Glorifying in having been raised up by God to be a scourge to the inequities and oppression of the age"(65). Exactly three years later, "Nemesis overtook Emperor Farrukhsiyar who had brutally murdered Banda and his companions. He was deposed, imprisoned, blinded and ultimately killed in a very ignominous manner on April, 28, 1719 C.E."(66).

"Thus died Banda Bahadur—a man who first chose to renounce the world to live in the peaceful seclusion of a sylvan hermitage, then renounced both pacificism and the life of solitude to rouse a downtrodden peasantry to take up arms; a man who shook one of the most powerful empires in the world to its very foundations with such violence that it was never again able to re-establish its authority"(67).

Banda's martyrdom can never be forgotten till the end of eternity. He sacrificed his all in the defence of his religion. Not the faintest groan escaped his lips even as he was being subjected to the most inhuman torture. Banda was one of the most remarkable men that India produced in the eighteenth century. "He was the first man who laid down the foundation of political sovereignty of the Sikhs. He had brought about a revolution in the minds of the people. He was a great national hero for the Hindus and the first empire builder of the Sikhs"(68).

Banda was a true Kshatriya, as he inherited the spirit of bravery, heroism, love of independence and self-sacrifice from his race. "His national and patriotic enthusiasm was further aroused by the Guru's sufferings and sacrifices, and ultimately by his death as a result of the Mughal Trickery"(69).

Some of the Sikh writers, however, unreservedly condemned Banda Singh for his introduction of the *Fateh Darshan*. Though he substituted *Fateh Darshan* (Victory to the faith) with *'Wahe Guru Ji Ka Khalsa'*, *'Wahe Guru Ji Ki Fateh'*, he never insisted upon his concept of *Fateh*

Darshan after its rejection by the *Khalsa*. Even after the slogan was withdrawn, many Sikhs were estranged. In his personal conduct as a Sikh, he was, throughout a devout follower of Sikhism, and his faith in the Gurus remained unshaken till his own martyrdom.

Architectural details: An overview

The building of the Gurdwara Banda Singh Bahadur located near Khwaja Qutab-Ud-Din Bakhtiyar Kaki Dargah (near Qutab Minar) at Mehrauli, was constructed only in 1991-92 by Late Baba Harbans Singh in memory of the martyrdom of Banda Singh Bahadur. According to Granthi Sardar Ranbeer Singh, the exact location of the site of the martyrdom of Baba Banda Singh Bahadur could be located only in 1980 by Sardar Avtar Singh, a Sikh scholar, who approached the Imam of Jama Masjid to show him the original documents and *Farman*s (royal orders) issued by the then Mughal Emperor of the execution of Banda Singh Bahadur. On careful scrutiny of the documents available at Jama Masjid, Delhi, Sardar Avtar Singh could find out the exact location of the place of Banda's martyrdom. It was stated to be just near the old large door adjacent to Khwaja Qutab-Ud-Din Bakhtiyar Kaki Dargah at Mehrauli. After much persuasion and payment of adequate local compensation, residents vacated the area identified as the place of Banda's martyrdom. The heavy stone walls on which two parts of the old wooden door were fixed are still there.

The martyrdom site is now transformed into a separate memorial structure adjoining the back portion of the recently constructed building of the Gurdwara. The place has a separate entrance for the visitors. The main building of the Gurdwara facing east does not exhibit any special architectural brilliance except that it is covered with white marble. The building is comparatively smaller in size; it has only one large-sized dome on the top on a flat base. The *Prakash Asthan* is also smaller in size but it is decorated with a few swords probably indicating Banda Singh Bahadur's undaunted valour and bravery. The hall on the ground floor is meant for special congregations or *Guru-ka-Langar*, arranged on special occasions.

Daily programmes

Gurdwara Baba Banda Singh Bahadur performs some daily programmes in order of the sequence mentioned below:

1. *Prakash* and *Hukamnama*: 2.20 a.m. to 2.30 a.m.
2. *Path Sukhmani Sahib*: 2.30 a.m. to 3.45 a.m.
3. *Nit Nem*: 3.45 a.m. to 4.45 a.m.
4. *Kirtan Asa-di-Var*: 5.00 a.m. to 7.30 a.m.
5. *Kirtan*: 8.45 a.m. to 2.30 p.m.
6. *Sodar* and *Rehras Sahib*: 6.45 p.m. to 7.15 p.m.
7. *Sohila* and *Sukhasan*: 10.00 p.m. to 10.15 p.m.

The number of visitors and devotees attending these daily programmes is comparatively low as the Gurdwara is situated in such a densely populated lane of Mehrauli that it is not easily accessible for the motorists.

The Gurdwara does not arrange for daily *Guru-ka-Langar* as the Delhi Sikh Gurdwara Management Committee has not yet accorded regular financial sanction for this service except on the last Saturday of every month.

The Gurdwara arranges singing of *Kirtan* two days a week, on Wednesdays and Sundays, in the morning from 8 a.m. However, on the last Saturday of every month, the Gurdwara arranges *Kirtan Darbar* in the morning hours from 7 a.m. to 10 a.m. The programme is attended by approximately 300-400 devotees and visitors from different areas of Delhi. The *Kirtan Darbar* accompanied by grade-1 musicians (*Ragis*) is considered to be one of the significant activities of the Gurdwara, though it is arranged only once in a month. The Gurdwara also arranges *Sangat* on every Sunday which is attended by an assembly of about 30 devotees.

Socio-cultural activity

The main cultural event of the Gurdwara is the yearly celebration on the occasion of Banda Singh's martyrdom day, which falls in the month of June. This day is popularly known as *Sahidi Divas* and it is celebrated on a large scale. A whole day programme is arranged in the Gurdwara complex, and a good number of devotees and visitors gather here to pay their homage to Banda Singh Bahadur.

Of all the historical Gurdwaras in Delhi, Gurdwara Baba Banda Singh Bahadur is not so well-known due to the following reasons:

That it is a historical site, but not a historical shrine sanctified by the visits of any of the Gurus.

That the place of Banda Singh Bahadur's martyrdom has been identified only recently, and the people are not so much aware of his achievements.

That there is no regular publicity programme or any other means to attract visitors, especially those who visit the adjoining historical monument, the Qutab Minar, or the historical shrine of Khwaja Qutab-Ud-Din-Bakhtiyar Kaki Dargah.

That there is no daily *Guru-ka-Langar* service. That the Gurdwara is not easily accessible for want of motorable roads.

While visiting the site of Banda Bahadur's martyrdom, one must bear in mind that Banda was the man chosen by Guru Gobind Singh to avenge the wrong done by the Mughal rulers. Guru Gobind Singh had diverted the attention of his followers from the plough to the sword. He had sown the seed, Banda reaped the harvest. The Guru had enumerated principles; Banda carried them into practice. The Guru had destroyed the awe inspired by Mughal deposition. Banda completely broke the chasm of its invincibility.

Delhi and the Sikhs During the Post-Guru Period

Delhi has been the centre of political activities from very early times, but it came into prominence in the twelfth century C.E. when it became the capital of Prithviraj Chauhan. Under the Sultanate, it enjoyed an exalted status. However, in the later half of the fourteenth century C.E., the last Sultan changed his capital from Delhi to Agra.

Again in 1526 C.E., Babur, the first Mughal Emperor re-established Delhi as the seat of his empire. But the city experienced a temporary diminution in its importance when the Mughal Emperors Akbar and Jahangir moved their headquarters from Delhi to Fatehpur Sikri and Agra. The city regained its importance when Shahjahan made it the headquarters of his empire, and since then it had enjoyed the status of being the headquarters of the Indian Government. The Sultans, the Mughals, the Marathas, the Jats and the Rajputs, all made attempts to occupy Delhi. The Sikhs also wanted to possess Delhi for certain reasons.

Even after the execution of Banda Singh Bahadur, the sufferings of the Sikhs did not end. They were persecuted by the Mughal Governors of Punjab. Eventually, another complicated factor was added to Punjab politics by the Afghan invasions of Ahmad Shah Abdali who was invited by Shah Nawaz Khan, the then Mughal Governor of Punjab to attack India.

Ahmad Shah Abdali launched his first attack on India in January, 1748 C.E. To meet this double danger of Mughal persecution and Afghan invasions, the Sikhs organized themselves into small military bands, about sixty-five in number, which pooled their resources in times of danger under the leaders like Nawab Kapur Singh and Jassa Singh Ahluwalia. The collective strength of these bands was called *Dal Khalsa* (Sikh Confederacy).

It was completely organized in 1748 C.E. Later on, these were amalgamated into a number of bigger units, about twelve in number which came to be called *Misl*s namely, Singpuria or Faizalpuria *Misl* (Founder: Nawab Kapur Singh), Ahluwalia *Misl* (Founder: Jassa Singh Ahluwalia), Bhangi *Misl* (Founder: Hari Singh), Ramgarhia *Misl* (Founder: Jassa Singh Ramgarhia), Kanheyia *Misl* (Founder: Jai Singh), Sukurchakiya *Misl* (Founder: Charat Singh), Phulkian *Misl* (Founder: Ala Singh), Dallewalia *Misl* (Founder: Gulab Singh), Nishanwalia *Misl* (Founder: Sangat Singh and Mohar Singh), Karorsinghia *Misl* (Founder: Bhagat Singh), Shahidi *Misl* (Founder: Baba Dip Singh), and Nakai *Misl* (Founder: Hira Singh).

These *Misl*s began to carve out principalities for themselves. The *Misldar*s looked like petty sovereigns. Though they used to fight against each other, they often combined to face the persecution of the Mughal Governors and to face the Afghan invasions. The main sources of income of the *Misldar*s were land revenue, *Rakhi* (one third of produce paid by the villagers), plunder, tribute (paid by the petty chiefs), import and export duties, and judicial proceedings (payment of *Nazrana* when stolen property was recovered and *Jurmana* when the party lost the case, and *Taikhana* when the case got prolonged).

In the course of time, the Sikh *Misl*s under the leadership of Jassa Singh Ahluwalia became very powerful in Punjab. They regained strength, and captured Lahore after killing the Afghan Governor. Ahmad Shah Abdali invaded India for the last time in 1767 C.E. He completely failed to crush the Sikhs.

After Ahmad Shah Abdali left India, the Sikh *Misl*s now planned their incursions on Delhi, the capital of the already declining Mughal Empire. The then Mughal Emperor Shah Alam II was merely a puppet in the hands of the English, his own ministers and the Marathas. The provincial governors were trying to grind their own axe. The Mughal Empire had politically and militarily become too weak to defend the country.

The Sikhs attacked Delhi not only for their sufferings in the hands of the tyrannical Mughal Governors of Punjab, but also for political reasons. For instance, they did not want to allow time to Delhi to organize aggression against them.

"The Sikhs undertook fourteen incursions on Delhi, and its suburbs in between April, 1766 and March, 1788 C.E."(70).

During their incursions, the Sikh revolutionaries had many opportunities to unfurl the Sikh flag at the Red Fort, but none of them went that way. Sardar Baghel Singh, the most daring and fearless *Misl* Chief of the Karorsinghia *Misl* entered the Mughal capital, Delhi, and stayed here for a long time with his strong army camped at Majnu-ka-Tilla and Tis Hazari, but he never availed of the opportunity to announce from the Red Fort, the formation of the Sikh Empire. As it appears, he was more interested in constructing Gurdwaras at various sites of the capital city.

The same can be said of other Sikh *Misl* Chiefs like Jassa Singh Ahluwalia, Jassa Singh Ramgarhia and Karan Singh who crossed the Yamuna many a time, and were given the chance to become the rulers of Hindustan, but they did not avail of the opportunity. Instead of capturing Delhi, they went over into the Doab and crossed the Ganges at several points. The *Misl* Chiefs could not plan for a united front during their incursions on Delhi. Moreover, they were often fighting against each other, and their main purpose during incursions was to amass booty by means of plundering the Mughal territories including the capital city of Delhi.

A painting showing Sikh soldiers led by Sardar Baghel Singh, Sardar Jassa Singh Ahluwalia and Sardar Jassa Singh Ramgarhia, who captured Delhi by defeating the Mughal forces and hoisted the Khalsa Flag on the Red Fort.

The causes of failure of the Sikhs to establish an Empire are not exactly known to us. They were no doubt capable soldiers, but their lackadaisical approach to such a great move perhaps did not yield any positive result. A close study of the Sikh *Misl*s will reveal that the *Misl* organization was a curious mixture of theocracy, democracy and absolutism. The Sikh soldiers and 'Sardars', all fought for their Guru.

When they assembled at Amritsar on certain occasions like *Diwali* and *Baisakhi*, they used to discuss the political problems and the common plan of action for the community. These meetings were

An imaginary painting (by Sardar Amreek Singh Panesar) showing Banda Singh Bahadur in the form of a warrior sitting in front of a fort.

called *Sarbatt Khalsa* (meeting of the entire body of the Sikhs). They passed resolutions in the presence of the *Guru Granth Sahib* and these resolutions were called *Gurmata* which means advice of the Guru. The *Misldar*s on these two occasions took their decisions in the presence of their followers.

It was democratic because every soldier or member of the *Misl* enjoyed social and political equality. But as there was no regular machinery to check the *Misl* groups, it was virtually absolutism. Moreover, there was no proper discipline in their army. Though the Sikhs organized themselves into armed bands (*Misl*s), they used to fight against each other. The subordinate Sikh Chiefs did not owe military or fiscal obligation to their Chiefs. They could easily transfer their services from one Chief to another.

As the *Misl* organization was a sort of feudal organization composed of divergent *Misl* bands without a supreme monarch or a Commander-in-Chief, the *Misl* Chiefs could not make any united effort to establish an Empire in the country. The main purpose of the Sikh *Misl*s was to fight against the then Mughal and Afghan rulers for their policies of persecution of the Sikhs.

The main outcome of the Sikh invasion of Delhi appears to be a far reaching change in the political condition of the country in the closing years of the eighteenth century C.E.

The time was favourable for Maharaja Ranjit Singh to expand his territory. Ranjit Singh was the son of Mahan Singh and grandson of Charat Singh of Sukurchakiya *Misl* which included the territories of Eminabad, Sialkot and Gurjanwala. After his father's death in 1792 C.E., Ranjit Singh became the ruler at the age of 12.

In the course of time, he became so powerful that he successfully effected the marvellous transformation of the warring Sikh states into a compact national monarchy. He initiated his military operations by conquering the Sikh *Misl*s who became weak due to their internal fighting.

The rulers of the declining Mughal and Afghan Empires became too weak to resist any incursions on their territories. Taking full advantage of the situation, Ranjit Singh annexed Lahore and Amritsar from Bhangi Sardars and also annexed Dallewalia *Misl*, Karorsinghia *Misl* and Faizalpuria *Misl* by 1811 C.E. By the year 1834 C.E., Ranjit Singh annexed Multan, Kangra, Kashmir, Ladakh, Peshawar and Dera Ghazi Khan.

He also conquered territories from the Muslim Chiefs as well as Hindu Rajas. Therefore, Maharaja Ranjit Singh created his own kingdom, and consolidated the Sikh military monarchy on the ruins of a waning *Misl* confederacy in Punjab.

Leaving aside the Sikh incursions on Delhi, the eighteenth century was a period of great significance in the growth of Sikhism. The Sikhs achieved great success in their struggle for assertion, identity, recognition and sovereignty. They could evolve new strategies and new institutions such as *Misaldari*, *Dal Khalsa*, *Rakhi* and *Gurmata* to cope with different challenges. "They also developed the theories and traditions of Sikh heroism and Sikh martyrdom. Moreover, they strove hard to make the idea of Panth-Guru as an integral part of the Sikh psyche"(71).

The history of Delhi from 1800 C.E. onwards is notable for the spread of the Crown rule, transfer of power from the East India Company to the Crown, and the period of the Indian Mutiny (1857 C.E.). The British had annexed most of the Indian states.

The Marathas, the Mughals, and the Rajputs, all had been humiliated by the British before the fall of Punjab. The victory over Punjab made them the supreme power in whole of India. Delhi came under their protection in 1803 C.E. In September, 1857 C.E., Brigadier Hudson captured Bahadur Shah II, Begum Zeenat Mahal, their three sons and a grandson. The three princes were stripped and were shot by Brigadier Hudson.

As it is known, the relationship of the British with the Sikhs of Delhi was cordial. An important outcome of the Indian Mutiny of

1857 C.E. was that the service in the armed forces was thrown open to the Punjabis, and specially the Sikhs. "The British Government had already provided that the Sikh fraternity would on no account be interfered with, and that the Sikhs should be permitted to wear their beard and turban as enjoined by their religion. Of the martial races, the favourites of the British Officers were the Sikhs and the Gurkhas" (72). It appears that the Sikhs enjoyed better social status under the British rule.

After the end of the Sikh rule in Punjab and with the advent of British rule in the country, the management and the maintenance of the Sikh shrines was passed on to the hands of the *Mahant*s under the religious endowment act of 1863 C.E. The simple forms of Sikh prayers and other services were transformed into complicated and extravagant ceremonies by the *Mahant*s. The *Mahant*s indulged in all sorts of vices, sometimes even heinous crimes were committed within the precincts of the Gurdwaras. The Sikhs, therefore, started to campaign vigorously to free their places of worship from the clutches of the *Mahant*s.

As a result, they got into a direct clash with the then British Government, and, for five years the Sikhs underwent countless sufferings inflicted on them by the *Mahant*s and the British Government.

On February 20, 1921, a batch of about 150 devotees came for obeisance at Nanakana Sahib Gurdwara (Sheikhupura district, 75 kilometres west-south-west of Lahore, Pakistan). Not only were they not allowed to enter the sacred shrine, but also the private army of *Mahant* Narain Das attacked them with arms and ammunition.

The attack was sudden and bullets were showered from all sides. Bhai Lachman Das, who had somehow managed to enter the shrine and was reciting the *Guru Granth Sahib*, was fired at. He died instantly with *Gurbani* on his lips. The holy book too was damaged and had strains of blood on it. Outside the main gate, the *Mahant* stood with a pistol in hand and directed the entire operation. Bhai Dalip Singh, said to be known to the *Mahant*, came forward and pleaded with him to stop the carnage. The *Mahant* turned a deaf ear to him and he was shot dead. Six other Sikhs who stood nearby were also killed by the *Mahant*'s men and were thrown in the potter's kiln, and burnt in open fire. A few others were tied to a tree and were burnt alive. The Nanakana Sahib Gurdwara outrage is perhaps unparalled for its barbarity in the history of mankind.

As the news of this ghastly episode spread, the whole country was shocked. It excited great sympathy for the Sikhs and there was a demand for drastic action against the *Mahant* and his henchmen. Representations were made to the Government.

The Governor of Punjab visited the place of incident and was deeply moved by the sight of the scene. Mahatma Gandhi also visited the place a few days later. The Government was forced to take action against the erring *Mahant* who was arrested with his hirelings. The Government handed over the management of the Gurdwara to a Committee of seven Sikhs.

But the matter did not end here. The Sikhs were deeply hurt by the desecration of the holiest of their holy places of worship and a wave of resentment spread. They could not forget the cruel and cold blooded murder of their brethren, and their hearts bled when they saw their holy book damaged.

On February 23, the dead bodies of the Sikh devotees were placed on the funeral pyre. The Sikhs remained calm. However, a protracted struggle and many *morcha*s later, the Government finally relented and the management of the affairs of the Gurdwaras was entrusted to the Sikhs.

The Sikh Gurdwara Act was passed on July 25, 1925, and the Gurdwara affairs were handed over to the Shiromani Gurdwara Prabandhak Committee.

The Shiromani Gurdwara Prabandhak Committee appointed a small committee consisting of Sardar Dan Singh Vachhoa as

Chairman, Sardar Gurdit Singh as Secretary and Sardar Harbans Singh Sistani, to enter into negotiations with the *Mahant*s and take over the management of the "Historical Gurdwaras of Delhi".

As the Sikh Gurdwaras Act gave the Shiromani Gurdwara Prabandhak Committee a statutary status and entrusted to it the management of all Gurdwaras affiliated to it through Government notification, the Shiromani Gurdwara Prabandhak Committee asked all the *Mahant*s of the "Historical Gurdwaras of Delhi" to hand over the management of these Gurdwaras to the Shiromani Gurdwara Prabandhak Committee.

Mahant Hari Singh of Gurdwara Sis Ganj Sahib was the first to hand over the Gurdwara and its property to the Committee on December 19, 1922. Other *Mahant*s except the *Mahant* of Majnu Tilla Sahib and Nanak Piau followed suit. The system of nomination of members to the local Managing Committee for Delhi Gurdwaras by the Shiromani Gurdwara Prabandhak Committee continued till 1937. Afterwards, the system of nomination by the Shiromani Gurdwara Prabandhak Committee to the local Managing Committee was made operative only in consultation with the Sikh *Sangat* (religious congregation) of Delhi. In 1945, a separate Gurdwara Committee, Delhi, was registered under the Societies Registration Act. This was superceded by the Delhi Sikh Gurdwara Management Committee established under section 3 of the Delhi Sikh Gurdwaras Act, 1971, passed by the Parliament.

A Gurdwara is the house of the Guru, where the Guru resides, and its doors opening out in four different directions, are thrown open to welcome people without any distinction of caste, class or creed. With no idol or image installed within the Gurdwara, it is dedicated to no particular deity, and offers a secular space to its visitors. The *Guru Granth Sahib* is not only the Holy Scripture of the Sikhs, it is almost like a Universal Holy Scripture of mankind, for its spirit is highly profound and there is nothing sectarian in it.

It includes hymns by the Sikh Gurus as well as those by Hindus, Muslims and the so-called untouchable saints and sages, whose hymns were in tune with the basic tenets of Sikhism. It is written in the spoken Punjabi language in the *Gurmukhi* script.

The noble sufferings and the supreme sacrifice of the Sikhs for the protection of their religion, their socio-cultural heritage, and for taking up the rightful causes of others, deserve to be appreciated by all of us. To make this world a better place to live in, we should always bear in mind, Guru Gobind Singh's immortal hymn:

Learn to love, be merciful, and forbear,
Be mild, be patient, have no lust,
Nor wrath, greed nor obstinacy.

Prakash Utsav of the Guru Granth Sahib

All the Gurdwaras in Delhi celebrated the 400th Anniversary of the *Prakash Utsav* of the *Guru Granth Sahib* on September 1, 2004. *Prakash Utsav* relates to the celebration of the very auspicious day on which the first installation of the *Guru Granth Sahib* (also called *Pothi Sahib*) took place in the Harimandir Sahib at the Golden Temple in Amritsar, and an old Sikh from Guru Nanak's time, Baba Budha was nominated as the first *Granthi*, the reader of the holy scripture. The first installation ceremony of the *Guru Granth Sahib* was held on August 16, 1604 C.E.

The Tenth Guru, Gobind Singh, before his death, took a momentous decision that there would be no human Gurus after him. He decreed that the *Granth Sahib*, the holy book containing the wisdom of the previous Gurus and the hymns of *Bhakt*s would be revered as the Guru from then on. The *Guru Granth Sahib* was now to be the friend, philosopher and guide of the faithful. He declared the *Guru Granth Sahib* as the ultimate authority on all matters pertaining to the Sikh religion.

Sikhism, therefore, became the only religion in which a book is revered as the Living Guru. The *Granth* enumerates the traits of the one Eternal Entity or *Akaal Purakh*, the one Supreme Soul or *Paramaatma* in a variety of ways starting with His traits in the *Mool Mantra*. It assures that all are His children. No one is a born sinner. Any one who loves Him can realize Him in their present life in human form. His

Page 155: *The Guru Granth Sahib encompasses the spiritual thoughts of the following Peers, Sufis and Bhagats belonging to different castes and religions.*

First Row: *Bhagat Surdas (Brahmin—Awadh), Bhagat Peepa (Brahmin—Gujarat), and Baba Sheikh Farid (Syed Muslim—Punjab)*

Second Row: *Bhagat Sain (Barber—Reva), Bhagat Namdev (Calico Printer—Maharashtra), and Bhagat Dhanna(Jat—Rajasthan).*

Third Row: *Bhagat Sadhna (Slaughter—Karachi, Sind), Bhagat Parmanand (Brahmin—Maharashtra) and Bhagat Bhikhan Shah (Muslim—U.P.).*

Fourth Row: *Bhagat Ravidas (Tanner/Cobbler—U.P.), Bhagat Kabir (Weaver—U.P.), and Bhagat Beni (Brahmin—Bihar).*

Fifth Row: *Bhagat Ramanand along with followers (Brahmin—Maharashtra), Bhagat Jai Dev (Brahmin—Bengal), and Bhagat Trilochan (Brahmin—Maharashtra).*

will prevails. Heaven and Hell are here around us, and we are in either of them, through our deeds. All days are the same, there are no specific auspicious days.

The *Guru Granth Sahib* is a unique collection of compositions of not only six Sikh Gurus, but of 15 *Bhakti* saints, 11 other learned writers or *Bhat*s and three Sikhs in 31 different *Raga*s. The other Gurus, namely, Guru Hargobind, Guru Har Rai, Guru Harkrishan, and Guru Govind Singh did not compose any hymn or verse which could be included in the *Guru Granth Sahib*. However, 59 hymns and 57 *Sloka*s of Guru Tegh Bahdur (the Ninth Guru) were included in the *Guru Granth Sahib*. Guru Nanak Devji alone composed 947 hymns, and these were included in the *Guru Granth Sahib* by Guru Arjan. Written in *Sant Bhasa* with *Gurmukhi* as the script used for transcription, the holy book was prepared by Guru Arjan, the Fifth Guru. Guru Arjan collected and systematically organized the *Banis* and compiled them into the *Guru Granth Sahib*. He also dictated the text of the Holy *Granth* to Bhai Gurdas, a devotee and a scribe, who prepared the first hand-written master copy. This *Granth* is called *Pothi Sahib* (original name of the *Guru Granth Sahib*). Words and phrases from Persian, Arabic, Hindi, Sanskrit and other Indian languages have been used. These compositions, which are devotional hymns and prayers to the 'Supreme', contain the message of love and devotion, truth, humility, mercy, brotherhood, equality, service to others and purity of mind and soul.

All volumes of the *Guru Granth Sahib* are respectfully called *Birs* (volumes, copies of the *Guru Granth Sahib*). There are conflicting views on the *Adi Granth*. The *Granth* installed in 1604 in the Golden Temple is believed to be in the possession of descendants of Guru Hargobind, the Sixth Guru, and is known as the "Kartarpur Bir". Then there is the "Damdama Bir" believed to be compiled by Guru Gobind Singh himself. This is the final version of the *Guru Granth Sahib* transcribed by Bhai Mani Singh, Guru Gobind Singh's devotee and scribe. It includes the *Bani* composed by the Ninth Guru Teg Bahadur. Bowing before this Holy *Granth* at Nanded on October 6, 1708 C.E.,

Guru Gobind Singh exhorted all Sikhs to accept the *Granth* as the Guru henceforth.

All 3,384 hymns consisting of 15,575 stanzas spread over 1,430 pages, are arranged under different *Raga*s or musical modes of the Indian classical music system as there is a strong belief that spiritual experiences can best be had through a combination of word and music like *Shabad-Kirtan* which creates an atmosphere of sanctity, and establishes a link between the Almighty and the devotee.

The sacred book is broadly organised into: (i) *Mool Mantra*, (ii) *Japji, Sodar, Rehras, Sohila,* (iii) *Bani*s of the Gurus, Saints, *Bhat*s and the Sikhs, chronologically under different *Raga*s, and, (iv) two *Shabads-Mundavani* or praise of the *Amrit Naam* and *Tera Keeta* or thanks to *Sat Guru*. At the very end, (v) *Raagmala* is incorprated.

All compositions included in it are treated as *Gurbani*—the Gurus' own words. Even today, no Sikh ceremony is regarded complete, unless it is performed in the presence of a *Granth*. The *Guru Granth Sahib* is kept on a raised platform under a canopy, covered with richly embroidered clothes in the Gurdwara. A *Granthi* or a *Sevadar*, remains in constant attendance and holds a *Chowri/Chavar* (a symbolic whisk of sovereignty) which he moves over the Holy book.

In the words of Pearl Buck, "It is a source book, an expression of man's loneliness, his aspirations, his longings, his cry to God and his hunger for communication with that being".

The world's smallest *Granth Sahib* is a complete miniature scripture, 2.5 cm wide and 2.5 cm tall, and is bound in gold. It was published in Germany close to 100 years ago. The miniatures were most probably created for the travelling Sikh devotees and pilgrims as well as for the soldiers of the Sikh Regiment when they went to war, as it could be easily carried. (Reference Kulbir Kaur and Jagmohan Singh: Times of India, New Delhi, dated 3.10.08 and 13.11.08)

Celebration of Guru Nanak's Birthday

Most of the Gurdwaras of Delhi celebrate the *Gurpurb*s, specially those related to the birthdays of the Gurus. Though the birthdays of these Gurus are celebrated with great enthusiasm, Guru Nanak's birthday is celebrated in such a grand scale that it assumes the significance of a festival of national importance. Guru Nanak was born to lead mankind from darkness to light. "He rejected the path of renunciation (Tyaga or Yoga), the authority of the Vedas and the Hindu caste system, emphasized the leading of a householder's life (Grihasthi), unattached to gross materialism" (Reference: Times of India, special page, no. 9, dated November, 15, 2005).

In Bhai Gurdas's words:

Guru Nanak hath appeared;
Lo! Mist hath vanished and light hath shown in the world.
Even as the Sun shines,
the stars disappear,
and darkness gets resplendent with light.

(Reference: S.S. Johar, *Handbook on Sikhism,* Delhi, 2003, pages 2-3).

The procession carrying the Guru Granth Sahib is also arranged in a small truck decorated with garlands and flowers, and a photograph of Guru Nanak.

Facing page: *Five armed guards who represent the Panj Piare (literally the five beloved ones), lead the procession carrying Nishan Sahibs (the Sikh flag).*

Guru Nanak's birthday is generally celebrated on the full-moon day of *Kartik* (October/November) every year. Two days before the anniversary, the *Guru Granth Sahib,* is taken up for *Akhand Path*. The reading carries on day and night without a break, from beginning to the end of the holy book. The main day of celebration starts with

On the day of Guru Nanak's birthday celebration, an early morning procession carrying the Guru Granth Sahib is arranged on a trolley-type carriage decorated with garlands and flowers.

Prabhat Pheris, early morning processions that begin from a particular *Gurdwara*, and then go around localities, singing *Shabad*s. On the day of the festival, the *Guru Granth Sahib* is also carried during the procession on a trolley-type carriage decorated with flowers. Five armed guards, who represent the *Panj Piare* (literally the five beloved ones), head the procession carrying *Nishan Sahibs* (the Sikh flag).

Local bands playing religious music also form a special part of the procession. A group of devoted women accompanying the procession sing hymns from the *Guru Granth Sahib*. School children marching to the tune of local bands are also a special feature of the procession. The route of the procession that follows is lined with devotees offering sweets and cold drinks to the procession members as well as the general public. The procession ends by returning to the Gurdwara, where a special *Guru-ka-Langar* is organized. All the people who visit the Gurdwaras on this day, sit together and share the traditional *Karah Prasad*.

Acrobatic performances are also arranged on the occasion of celebration of the birthdays of any of the Gurus.

While celebrating Guru Nanak's birthday, we should bear in mind that Guru Nanak's basic concepts of Sikhism are mainly concerned with the services of mankind (*Kar-Seva*), *Kirtan* (singing of scriptural hymns), *Satsang* (religious gathering) and faith in 'one' omnipotent God who is infinite. According to him, God is formless (*Nirankar*), one soul, invisible, self-existent, incomprehensible, timeless, all pervading, indescribable and creator of all things (*Karta Purakh*).

On Guru Nanak's birthday the best tribute to this founder father of Sikhism should be to remember him for his great contribution for the social and spiritual upliftment of mankind. His teachings are as relevant in today's world as they were during his earthly presence in the fifteenth century C.E.

Glossary

Adi Granth	The first or primary *Granth*. Presently known as *Guru Granth Sahib*, the Holy Scripture of the Sikhs (abbreviated A.G.).
Akal Purakh	Eternal Entity.
Akhand Jyoti	Non-stop burning of flame in a place of worship.
Akhand Path	Non-stop reading of the complete text of *Guru Granth Sahib*.
Allah	The Arabic word for 'God'.
Amrit	Nectar; water sweetened and stirred in a steel bowl with *khanda* (double-edged sword with curved sides and pointed end) to the accompaniment of recital of certain prescribed scriptural texts in turn by five baptized Sikhs (*panj piare*) used in the initiation ceremony of the *khalsa* (brotherhood or community of Sikhs, especially of baptized Sikhs and practising Sikhs).
Amrit Sarovar	Sacred tank filled with nectar.
Anand	Greatest spiritual bliss.
Ardas	Supplication; supplicatory prayer of the Sikhs.
Baentee Chaupai	A hymn composed by Guru Gobind Singh which is included in the *Rehras* (Evening/Dusk time prayer).
Bairagi	A Shaivite cult of Hindu ascetics, any member of such cult.
Baisakhi	A festival held on the first of the *Vikrami* month of *Baisakh*.
Bandais	The companions of Banda Singh Bahadur.
Bangla	Bungalow.
Bani	Utterance, scriptural hymns or texts, same as *Gurbani*.
Baniya	A merchant, a trader, a shop-keeper.

Bhakt	A worshipper, a devotee.
Bhakti	Faith, worship, belief.
Bhat	A bird, a ministrel.
Bhog	Food formally placed in front of *Guru Granth Sahib* for God's blessings.
Brahman	A person belonging to the first of the four castes among the Hindus.
Chadar	A sheet, a coverlet.
Chhauni	A tent, a military camp.
Chola	A long robe.
Chowri/Chavar	A symbolic whisk of sovereignty.
Chubacha	A reservoir of water.
Chubara	An open space or room built under the roof of a house, an attic.
Dal Khalsa	The collective strength of the Sikh bands (*Misl*s) was called *Dal Khalsa* (Sikh confederacy) in the middle of the eighteenth century C.E.
Damdama	Temporary resting place, halting place.
Darbar	Court, Guru's Court; Gurdwara.
Darbar Sahib	*Guru Granth Sahib*; name for some important Gurdwaras, particularly the holy complex at Amritsar comprising the holy tank, *Harimandir, Akal Takht* and other shrines.
Darshan	Sight, glimpse.
Darwaza	A door.
Dewan	Congegration, Royal Assembly, a Minister, a Superintendent.
Dharamsal	Place of worship; Gurdwara.
Dharma	Religion.
Dohira	A hymn composed by Guru Gobind Singh which is included in the *Rehras* (Evening/Dusk time prayer).
Fakir	Mahammedan mendicant, a hermit, a recluse.
Farman	Royal edict, Royal order.
Fateh Darshan	Victory to the faith.
Faujdar	Garrison Commander, Officer ruling over a *sircar* (during the Mughal Period).
Gaddi/Gurgaddi	Seat of the Guru, Guru's throne, pontificate.
Granthi	Scripture reader as well as the caretaker of the Gurdwara.

Grihasthi	House-holder's life.
Gumti	A bastion, tower.
Gurbani	Utterance of hymns composed by the Gurus; text of *Guru Granth Sahib*.
Gurbilas	Biography of a Guru in verse.
Gurdwara	A Sikh place of worship; literally a Guru's door, threshold, house or abode.
Gurmat	Tenets of Sikh faith, Sikh theology.
Gurmata	Resolution, plan for action approved by *Sangat* or *Sarbatt Khalsa* in the presence of the *Guru Granth Sahib*.
Gurmat Vidyalaya	Teaching Centre for learning of tenets of Sikh faith, Sikh theology.
Gurmukhi	A script invented by Guru Nanak; the Punjabi language is written in this script.
Guru/Guruji	Spiritual teacher/Guide.
Gurpurb	Celebration of birthday anniversary related with Guru's life.
Guru-Granth-Sahib	Also known as *Adi Granth*, the Holy scripture of the Sikhs.
Guru Itihas Katha	Historical tales about the Guru*s*.
Guru-ka-Langar/ Langar	Free or joint community meal especially one arranged in Gurdwaras common kitchen attached to or run by Gurdwaras.
Guruship	One who holds position of a Spiritual Preceptor in Sikhism.
Gyani	Learned, possessing religious wisdom.
Haj	A pilgrimage to Mecca.
Harimandir	Literally temple of God; also known as the Golden temple, Amritsar to the English-speaking world.
Haveli	A large fortified mansion.
Hola Mohalla	The festival of the spring season held in March, the day after *Holi*.
Holi	Festival of colours celebrated on the last day of the bright half of *Phalgun* (March).
Hukam	Order, command; Divine will.
Hukamnama	Written order, letter issued by the Guru or from one of the *takhts* containing an order, judgement, proclamation.
Imam	A chief, a priest, a prelate.
Jagir	Rent-free grant given by Government as a reward for some services.
Jamdhar	A type of dagger.

Janamsakhi	Biography, especially one of the early biographical-cum-hagiographical accounts of Guru Nanak Dev's life.
Japji	A composition of 38 hymns with two *slokas*, the first and the last. It was composed by Guru Nanak.
Jazia	Pilgrimage tax imposed on the Hindus by the Muhammedan kings.
Jurmana	Fine, penalty.
Kalgi	A prince's feather plume, crest, an ornament for the head.
Karaha	Cauldron.
Karahprasad	Consecrated pudding of wheat-flour, sugar and clarified butter. It is distributed among the devotees in a Gurdwara.
Karamat	Miracle.
Karma	Work, deed.
Karseva	Free voluntary labour especially for construction/reconstruction of Gurdwara building or for digging, desilting, and cleaning of *Sarovars* (sacred bathing tank usually attached to Gurdwaras).
Karsevawale	Engaged in *Karseva.*
Karta Purakh	Creator of all things.
Katar	Dagger.
Katha	Religious discourse.
Kazi	A Muhammedan judge or law-officer.
Khalsa/Khalsa-Panth	The entire body, brotherhood or community of Sikhs.
Khanda	Double-edged sword with curved sides and a pointed end.
Khande-da-Amrit/ Khande-di-pahul	Intiation ceremony of the *Khalsa.*
Khangah	Community kitchen.
Khanjar	Paniard.
Khillat	Gift of honour bestowed by a King.
Kirpan	A small sword, a scimitar.
Kirtan	Singing of scriptural hymns, devotional music.
Kirtan Darbar	Singing of scriptural hymns/ devotional music in a congregation.
Kotwal	Police Commissioner in a city or town.
Kotwali	Police Station in a city or town.

Kshatriya	A person belonging to the second of the four castes among the Hindus.
Kubera/Kuvera	The god of wealth, the Mammon of Hindu mythology.
Langar	Free community meal arranged in Gurdwaras, same as *Guru-ka-Langar*.
Mahant	Head priest of a Gurdwara.
Majnu-ka-Tilla	Hillock of Majnu, the Muslim *Sufi Fakir* from Iraq.
Manji	Missionary centre originally established by Guru Nanak. Guru Amar Das set up twenty-two *Manjis* in different parts of the country each under the charge of a pious Sikh with whose effort the Sikh *Sangats* (congregations) met daily and chanted the Guru's hymns. This was done with a purpose of spreading the message of Sikhism as propagated by Guru Nanak.
Manji Sahib	An architectural design of a *Prakash Asthan* (sanctum) consisting of a small, low-roofed structure usually about three metre square where *Guru Granth Sahib* is seated.
Masand	Guru's agent-cum-preacher appointed during the time of the Fourth Guru. Guru Gobind Singh (the tenth Guru), however, abolished the institution shortly before the creation of *Khalsa* in the year 1699 C.E.
Mela	Crowd, assemblage, fair.
Misl	The Arabic word *Misl* means equal. Any of the twelve divisions of the *Dal Khalsa*, the confederate army of the Sikhs during the latter eighteenth century C.E.
Misldari	Any *Misldar* (Head of a *Misl*) having his own principalities called *Misldari* in the latter eighteen century C.E.
Morcha	Literally trench, fortification, battle or war front, agitation, confrontation.
Mullah/Maulvi	A learned Muhammedan (one who is equally versed in Arabic and Persian literature).
Nam	Literally name, God's Name.
Nazrana	Present, a gift.
Neem	Margosa tree, *Azadirachta Indica*.
Nihang	A sect of baptized, ever ready, heavily armed Sikhs, a member of this sect or one dressed and equipped in this manner; a member of *Buddha Dal* or *Taruna Dal* into which *Nihang*s are organized.
Nirankar	Formless.

Nishan Sahib	The Sikh flag or standard, triangular in shape and saffron in colour except in the case of *Nihangs* who have a dark blue flag. *Nishan Sahib* is the essential distinguishing feature of a Gurdwara.
Nit Nem	*Nit Nem* is daily discipline of reciting the set of five *Bani*s (scriptures) prescribed by the Gurus. It includes recitation of morning, evening and bedtime prayers.
Pahar	The eighth part of a day, a period of three hours.
*Pahari Raja*s	*Raja*s of the hilly areas of North India.
Pahul	Baptism, initiation ceremony.
Pandit	A very wise or intelligent person.
Pangat	Row, line for serving *Guru-ka-langar*.
Panj Piare	The first five Sikhs who came forward at Guru Gobind Singh's call at Anandpur Sahib on March 30, 1699 for any sacrifice, the Guru named them *Panj Piare* (literally the five beloved ones). The Guru administered *khande- di- pahul* (initiation ceremony of the *Khalsa*) to them and then asked them to likewise baptize him. Since then any five baptized, practising, pious Sikhs selected to conduct the baptism ceremony of the *Khalsa* or for other ceremonial occasions such as leading a procession or inaugurating *karseva*, have been called *Panj Piare.*
Panth	Religious community; the Sikh community.
Paramaatma	Supreme Soul.
Parikrama	Circumambulation.
Path	Reading of scriptural texts.
Pati	Self respect, honour.
Piau	Deep well for serving cold drinking water to the thirsty passers by.
Pipal	*Ficus religiosa*, a kind of tree considered sacred by the Hindus.
Pothi Sahib	First hand- written master copy of the Holy *Granth.*
Prabhat Pheri	Early morning procession.
Prakash	Open state of the *Guru Granth Sahib.*
Prakash Asthan	Sanctum, the place where the *Guru Granth Sahib* is seated.*Prakash Utsav* Celebration of the first installation of the *Guru Granth Sahib* at the Golden temple in Amritsar.

Prasad	Offering of food to *Sri Guru Granth Sahib* and then taking of the offered food as the blessing of the divinity.
Puran	Ancient tale of bygone ages, Hindu mythology/mythical traditions.
Puratan	Old, ancient
Qalendar	Muslim anchorite.
Qazi	A Mohammedan Judge or Law-officer.
Quran	The sacred book of the *Mohammedans.*
Raga	A musical mode.
Ragis	Musicians.
Raja	A king , lord , a monarch, a sovereign.
Rakab	Stirrup.
Rakhi	A system under which one-third of produce paid by the villagers to the *Misldars* called *Rakhi.*
Rehras	Evening/Dusk time Prayer; a collection of hymns of five different Gurus. The theme of the hymns is the description of the house of God and the mode to enter it.
Sachkhand	Literally region of Truth.
Sadhu	Hermit.
Sahib	An honorofic suffix.
Sahidi	Martyrdom; concerning martyrdom.
Sahidi Divas	Martyrdom day.
Sahidi jatha	Band of volunteers vowed to do or die
Sajjadanashin	Caretaker of a Mausoleum.
Samadhi	Memorial built over the ashes of a deceased person.
Samvat/(Vikrami)	An era, the year of Vikram era; Vikramaditya, the celebrated king of Ujjain founded an era which commenced from mid March 57 B.C. (i.e. 57 years prior to the Christian era)
Sangat/Sat Sangat	Company; religious congregation; body of worshippers assembled in a Gurdwara.
Sant	Saint, particularly one believing in the one Transcendent God.
Sarai	Accommodation for the pilgrims.
Sarbatt Khalsa	A Sikh institution, a special assembly representing the entire *Khalsa Panth.*

Sarovar	Sacred bathing tank usually attached to the Gurdwaras.
Seva	Self-less service, especially voluntary and free service; same as *Kar-seva.*
Sevadar	Volunteer, one who offers voluntary and free service.
Shabad	A sacred scriptual hymn.
Shabad-ka-Langar	Offering of Guru's blessings through recitation of sacred scriptual hymns to the devotees who come to a Gurdwara for participation in worship and prayer through established practices such as organized *Kirtan* and *Katha* (interpretation of the Sikh scriptures).
Shia	Division, sect; fundamentally as a nick name, to a smaller branch of Islam than the *Sunnis.*
Sodar	Singing of scriptural hymns in praise of God in the evening.
Sohila	Singing of scriptual hymns in praise of god before going to bed.
Sudra	A person belonging to the fourth of the four castes among the Hindus.
Sufi	Muslim mystic; in India often closely linked with non-Muslim ascetic traditions.
Sukhasan	An easy-chair, a couch; a palanquin.
Sukhmani Sahib	The psalm of peace, its aim is to give solace to the mind. There are 24 cantos in this composition; Guru Arjan was the composer of *Sukhmani.*
Sunni	The main body of the Muslims. They claim to be followers of Muhammad, and to be the real community.
Swayya	A hymn composed by Guru Gobind Singh which is included in the *Rehra*s (Evening/Dusk time prayer).
Tabla	A type of Tambourine.
Takht/Takht Sahib	Literally throne; any of the five Gurdwaras recognized as the highest seat of religious authority for the Sikhs, *namely Sri Akaal Takht Sahib, opposite the Harimandir (Golden Temple), Amritsar; Takht Sri Harimandir Sahib at Patna Sahib, Patna, Bihar; Takht Sri Keshgarh Sahib at Anandpur Sahib, District Ropar, Punjab; Takht Sachkhand Sri Hazoor Sahib Abichal Nagar, Nanded, Maharashtra, and Takht Sri Damdama Sahib, Talwandi Sabo village, District Bhatinda, Punjab.*
Tat Khalsa	The main body of the Sikhs.
Tir	Arrow.

Tirsthan	The exact spot in the Moti Bagh Gurdwara complex from where Guru Gobind Singh shot two arrows into the Red Fort.
Tirtha	A sacred place, a place of pilgrimage, a holy spot.
Tyaga	Renunciation.
Udasi	Literally sadness, lonesomeness; a sect of unbaptised Sikh *Sadhus,* a member of this sect; travel, odyssey especially those undertaken by Guru Nanak Dev.
Vaishya	A person belonging to the third of the four castes among the Hindus.
Vak	Recitation of a hymn from *Guru Granth Sahib* opened at random.
Valmiki	Name of a low caste falling in the category of sweepers.
Vikrami	An Indian era or calendar commencing from mid March 57 B.C.
Yaksha	A kind of demi-god, attendant on *Kubera* employed to guard his gardens and treasure.
Yatri	A pilgrim, a traveller, a passenger, a tourist.
Yogi	Practitioner of *Yoga* (profound meditation).
Zamindar	Proprietor of landed estate, landholder, a landlord.
Zil-e-Ilahi	Shadow of God on earth.

End Notes

- Tobacco, Narcotics, and intoxicants such as hemp, opium, liquor, cocaine, etc. in any shape or form are not to be carried into the Gurdwara premises.
- *Shoe*s including *shock*s, *stick*s and *umbrella*s of visitors are to be left outside the holy premises. They are taken care of by the Gurdwara employees free of charge.
- Visitors will please wash their hands and feet at the taps at the entrance outside the holy grounds.
- Visitors will please keep their heads covered as long as they are inside the Gurdwara complex.

The Sikh Gurus

Guru	The then Rulers in Delhi	Place of Birth	Birth	Death
Nanak (I)	Bahlol Lodhi 1451-89 C.E. Sikander Lodhi 1489-1517 C.E. Ibrahim Lodhi 1517-26 C.E. Babar 1526-30 C.E. Humayun 1530-40 C.E.	Village Talwandi now known as Nankana Sahib (Pakistan).	15.4.1469	22.9.1539
Angad (II)	Humayun Sher Shah Suri 1540-56 C.E.	Village Matte-di-Sarai, Firozpur District, Punjab.	31.3.1504	29.3.1552
Amar Das (III)	Humayun Sher Shah Suri 1555-56 C.E. Akbar 1556-1605 C.E.	Village Basarke, District Amritsar, Punjab.	5.5.1479	1.9.1574
Ram Das (IV)	Akbar	Lahore (now in Pakistan).	24.9.1534	1.9.1581
Arjan Dev (V)	Akbar Jahangir 1605-1627 C.E.	Goindwal (situated on the right bank of Beas river), District Amritsar, Punjab.	15.4.1563	30.5.1606
Hargobind (VI)	Jahangir Shah Jahan 1627-1658 C.E.	Village Wadali, District Amritsar, Punjab.	14.6.1595	3.3.1644
Har Rai (VII)	Shah Jahan Aurangzeb 1658-1707 C.E.	Kiratpur, District Ropar, Punjab.	26.2.1630	30.6.1661
Harkrishan (VIII)	Aurangzeb	Kiratpur, District Ropar, Punjab.	7.7.1656	30.3.1664
Teg Bahadur (IX)	Aurangzeb	Holi city of Amritsar, Punjab.	1.4.1621	11.11.1675
Gobind Singh (X)	Aurangzeb Bahadur Shah 1707-1712 C.E.	Patna, Bihar.	22.12.1666	7.10.1708

References Cited

1. J.D. Cunningham, *A History of the Sikhs*, First published in 1849: Reprinted 1972, Delhi, p.34.
2. J.P. Suda, *Religions in India-A Study of their Essential Unity*. Sterling Publishers Pvt. Ltd, New Delhi, 1978, pp. 225-227. See also Col. D.S.Grewal, *Guru Nanak's Travel to Himalayan and East Asia Region: A New Light,* National Book Shop, Chandni Chowk, Delhi, 1995, p.5.
3. *Var Majh*. See also Surinder Singh Johar (S.S. Johar), *The Sikh Gurus and Their Shrines,* Delhi, 1976, p.37.
4. Indubhushan Banerjee, *Evolution of the Khalsa,* Vol. I, Foundations of the Sikh Panth, University of Calcutta, 1936, p.50.
5. Macauliffe, M.A. *The Sikh Religion*, Vol. I, p.5.
6. *Guru Granth Sahib*, p.39.
7. Col. D.S. Grewal, *op. cit*, pp.5-9
8. Surjit Singh Gandhi, *History of the Sikh Gurus (A Comprehensive Study),* Gur Das Kapur and Sons(P) Ltd, Delhi-Jullundur-Ghaziabad, First Edition, 1978, pp.91-92.
9. Major Gurmukh Singh (Retd), *Historical Sikh Shrines,* Singh Brothers, Amritsar, 1995, pp.279-280.
10. Surinder Singh Johar, *The Sikh Gurus and Their Shrines,* Vivek Publishing Company, Kamla Nagar, Delhi, 1976, pp.80-81.
11. Dr. Trilochan Singh, Chapter on: *Historical Sikh Shrines in Delhi,*

Delhi Sikh Gurdwara Board, Sis Ganj, Chandni Chowk, Delhi, 1972, p.21.

12. S.S. Johar, *op.cit.* p.46.
13. Vivek Ranjan Bhattacharya, *Secular Thoughts of the Sikh Gurus*, With a Foreword by Giani Zail Singh, Gian Publishing House, Delhi, 1988, pp.126-127.
14. Patwant Singh, '*The Guru and the Granth: A View through World's Gurdwaras,*' The Tribune, February 21, 1993.
15. G.S. Dhillon, *Insights into Sikh Religion and History,* Singh and Singh Publishers, Chandigarh, 1991,p.12 (Essentials of Sikhism).
16. *Guru Granth Sahib*: 642.
17. *Guru Granth Sahib*, p.1424.
18. Dr. S.S. Kapoor, *The Religion and the Sikh people,* Hemkunt Press, New Delhi, 1992, "*The Sikh Theology*, Part VII, Unit 19, pp. 179-180.
19. Dr. Trilochan Singh, op.cit, pp.22-24. See also S.S. Johar, op.cit, p.127.
20. Macauliffe, M.A., *op.cit*, Vol.III, P.99.
21. Indubhushan Banerjee, *Evolution of the Khalsa,* Vol.II, p.7.
22. Trumpp Earnest, *The Adi Granth*, p. XXXII.
23. Surinder Singh Johar, *op.cit*, p. 64.
24. Mohsin Fani, *Debistan Muzahib,* translated by D. Shea A. Troyer and Ganda Singh. Also vide S.S. Johar *op.cit*, p.65.
25. J.D. Cunnigham, *op.cit*, p.32.
26. R.S. Wahiwala. "*Kirtan* (*Devotional music*)", SB. No. 6, 1989, p.18.
27. J. Singh Salna, "*Importance of Kirtan in Gurmat*". SC I, Vol.32, No.74, 1992, p.12.
28. Merv Fowler, *Sikhism in World Religions,* Edited by Sussex Academic Press, 1997, p.361.
29. Taran Singh, *Japu Darshan Didar*, Faqir Singh and Sons, Amritsar, p.46.
30. Sharad Chandra Verma, *Guru Nanak and the Logos of Divine*

Manifestation, Delhi Gurdwara Prabandhak Committee, 1967, p.396.

31. Avtar Singh, *Ethics of the Sikhs,* Patiala, Punjabi University, 1970, pp.30-31.
32. Gurnam Kaur, *Reason and Revelation in Sikhism,* Cosmo Publications, New Delhi, 1990, pp.144-149.
33. Dr. S.S. Kapoor, *op.cit.* pp.169-170.
34. Dr. Trilochan Singh, "*Fundamental Beliefs of Sikh Religion,*" Delhi Sikh Gurdwara Board, 1972, pp.58-59. See also W. Owen Cole and Piara Singh Sambhi, *The Sikhs: Their Religious Beliefs and Practices,* Vikas Publishing House Pvt. Ltd., New Delhi, 1978, pp.171-173.
35. M.A. Macauliffe, *op.cit,* Vol. V, P.93.
36. Dr. Trilochan Singh, *op.cit,* pp.24-25.
37. Guru Gobind Singh: *Dasam Granth.* See also Dr. Trilochan Singh, *op.cit,* p26.
38. Dr.Trilochan Singh, op.cit, pp.24-25. See also S.S. Johar, *op.cit.* pp.195-196 and Gurmukh Singh, *op.cit,* pp.280-281.
39. *Guru Granth Sahib*, p.185 and p.1245.
40. Dr.Trilochan Singh, *Fundamental Beliefs of Sikh Religion, op.cit,* p.55.
41. *Guru Granth Sahib.*
42. Dr.Trilochan Singh, *op.cit.* p.27.
43. *Bachiter Natak.* See also Dr. Trilochan Singh, op.cit, p.30 and S.S. Johar, *op.cit.* p.230.
44. J.D. Cunningham, *op.cit.* p.58.
45. Surjit Singh Gandhi, *"Nanak IX-Guru Tegh Bahadur"*, in *History of the Sikhs And Their Religion*, Vol. I, Edited by Kirpal Singh and Kharak Singh, Shiromani Gurdwara Prabandhak Committee, Amritsar, 2004, pp.242-43. See also *The Encyclopaedia of Sikhism*, Edited by Prof Harbans Singh, Punjabi University, Patiala, Vol. IV, *'Tegh Bahadur, Guru,'* p.332.
46. S.S.Johar, *op.cit.* p.230;

47. *Bachiter Natak*. See also S.S. Johar, *op.cit.* p.230.
48. Indubhushan Banerjee, *op.cit.*, Vol. II, pp.60-61.
49. Raj Khalsa 30-32; Forest's Selections III, 1124, Dilliyethi p.1,84; Hari Ram Gupta, *History of the Sikhs II*, p.143.
50. See also S.S. Johar, op.cit. p 231. See also Gurmukh Singh,*op.cit.* p.280. See also Harbans Singh Chawla, *Sardar Baghel Singh*, Delhi Sikh Gurdwara Management Committee, 2001.
51. Dr. Trilochan Singh,op.cit.pp.31-33.
52. S.S.Johar,op.cit.p.232. See also Harbans Singh Chawla, *Sardar Baghel Singh*, *op.cit.*, 2001.
53. Ganda Singh, *A Brief Account of the Sikh People,* Delhi Sikh Gurdwara Management Committee, Delhi, 1988, p.64.
54. Mohammad Latif, *A History of the Punjab, Calcutta, 1891,* p.270.
55. *Bachiter Natak*, chapter-6.
56. Dr.Trilochan Singh, *op.cit.* pp.35-36. See also S.S. Johar, op.cit. pp.293-295; Gurmukh Singh,op.cit.p.281.
57. Pritam Singh Gill, *Heritage of Sikh Culture,* New Academic Publishing Co. Jullundur, 1975, pp.92-93.
58. S.S.Johar, op.cit. p.292.
59. Dr. Trilochan Singh.*op.cit.* pp.36-37.
60. Dr. Trilochan Singh, *op.cit,* p.37.
61. Guru Gobind Singh, *Akal Ustat*,86.
62. Mohammed Latif, *op.cit.* p.239.
63. Dr. S.S. Kapoor, *op.cit.* pp.194-198 (Rise and fall of Banda Bahadur). See also Harbans Singh Chawla, *Banda Singh Bahadur De Antley Din*, Delhi Sikh Gurdwara Management Committee, June, 1996.
64. Ganda Singh, *Life of Banda Singh Bahadur (Based on Contemporary and Original Records),* Publication Bureau, Punjabi University, Patiala, 1999, Chapter XIX (Massacre of the Sikhs and Banda Singh Bahadur at Delhi), pp.146-147.
65. Mounts Taurt Elphinstone, *An Account of the Kingdom of Cabul,*

2 Vols. London,1896.

66. Dr. Trilochan Singh, *Historical Sikh Shrines in Delhi, op.cit.* pp.39-40.
67. Mohammed Latif, *op.cit.* p.279.
68. Piara Singh Data, *Banda Singh Bahadur*, National Book Shop, Chandni Chowk, Delhi, pp.78-79.
69. S.S. Johar, *The Sikh Sword to Power*, ARSEE Publishers, Delhi, 2002, p.37.
70. Surjit Singh Gandhi, *Sikhs in the Eighteenth Century,* Singh Brothers, Amritsar, 1979, pp.577-581.
71. Dr. S.S. Kapoor, *The Sikh Religion and the Sikh People,* 1992, *op.cit.* p.244.
72. Surjit Singh Gandhi; op.cit.p.624.

Picture Credits

Shri Anoop Asthana (courtesy): Delhi Sikh Gurdwara Management Committee): 2, 10, 11, 23, 26, 27, 28, 32, 35, 36, 40, 41, 42, 55, 56, 57, 58, 63, 64, 68, 69, 70, 73, 76, 77, 78, 86, 88, 89, 91, 92, 93, 97, 99, 102, 103, 104, 108, 109, 110, 111, 112, 115, 116, 118, 119, 120, 126, 129, 132, 135, 137 and 161

Sardar Amreek Singh Panesar (PAN Multimedia, Noida): 5, 8, 14, 16, 25, 31, 33, 44, 52, 60, 79, 82, 83, 94, 105, 122, 130, 131, 134, 145, 146 and 147.

Sardar Amreek Singh Panesar (PAN Multimedia, Noida): 155 (Courtesy Punjab and Sindh Bank, Delhi)

M.K. Pal: 107

Shri Anil Bhatia, General Secretary, Gurdwara Sri Guru Singh Sabha (Regd.), Pocket-G, Sarita Vihar, New Delhi76: 158, 159 and 160.

Bibliography

1. Avtar Singh: *Ethics of the Sikhs*, Punjabi University, Patiala, 1970.
2. Chawla, Harbans Singh: *Baba Banda Singh Bahadur De Antley Din*, Delhi Sikh Gurdwara Management Committee, Delhi, June, 1996: *Sardar Baghel Singh*, Delhi Sikh Gurdwara Management Committee, 2001: *Sri Guru Harkrishan Sahibji*, Delhi Sikh Gurdwara Management Committee, 2005.
3. Cole, W.O: *The Guru in Sikhism*, London, Darton, Longman and Todd, 1982.
4. Cole, W.O and Sambhi, Piara Singh: *The Sikhs, Their Religious Beliefs and Practices*, Vikas Publishing House, New Delhi, 1978.
5. Cunnigham, J.D: *A History of the Sikhs*, S.Chand and Co. (Pvt) Ltd, Reprinted 1972, New Delhi, (First published in 1849).
6. Data, Piara Singh: *Banda Singh Bahadur*, National Book Shop, Delhi.
7. Dharam Singh (Ed.); *Sikhism and Secularism*, Essays in honour of Prof. Harbans Singh, Harman Publishing House, New Delhi, 1994.
8. Dilgeer, Harjinder Singh: *Dictionary of Sikh Philosophy*, Sikh University Press, 2004.
9. Dilgeer, Harjinder Singh : *The Sikh Reference Book*, 1997.
10. D.S. Grewal: *Guru Nanak's Travel to Himalayan and East Asia Region: A New Light*, National Book Shop, Chandni Chowk, Delhi, 1995.
11 Fauja Singh: *Travels of Guru Govind Singh*, Punjabi University, Patiala, 1968
12. Ganda Singh: *Life of Banda Singh Bahadur* (Based on contemporary and original Records), Publication Bureau, Punjabi University, Patiala, 1999.
13. Ganda Singh: *A Brief Account of the Sikh People*, Delhi Sikh Gurdwara Management Committee, Delhi, 1988.

14. Gurmukh Singh: *Historical Sikh Shrines*, Singh Brothers, Amritsar, First Edition, 1995.
15. Gurnam Kaur: R*eason and Revelation in Sikhism*, Cosmo Publications, New Delhi, 1990.
16. G.S. Dhillon: *Insights into Sikh Religion and History*, Singh and Singh Publishers, Chandigarh, 1991.
17. Harbans Singh: *Guru Nanak and Origions of Sikh Faith*, Asia Publishing House, New Delhi, 1969.
18. Harbans Singh: *The Heritage of the Sikhs*, Manohar Publications, New Delhi, 1983.
19. Hari Ram Gupta: *History of the Sikh Gurus,* U.C. Kapur and Sons, New Delhi, 1973
20. Indubhushan Banerjee: *Evolution of the Khalsa*, Vol.I, Foundations of the Sikh Panth, University of Calcutta, 1936.
21. Johar, S.S: *The Sikh Gurus and Their Shrines*, Vivek Publishing Company, Delhi, 1976.
22. J.P. Suda: *Religions in India-A Study of their Essential Unity*, Sterling Publishers, New Delhi, 1978.
23. J. Singh Sarna: "*Importance of Kirtan in Gurmat*", SCI, Vol.32, No. 74, 1992.
24. Kashmir Singh: *Law of Religious Institutions-Sikh Gurdwaras*, Guru Nanak Dev University, Amritsar, 1989.
25. Mehr Singh: *Sikh Shrines in India*, Publication Division, Min. of Information & Broadcasting, New Delhi, 1975.
26. Merv Fowler: *Sikhism in World Religions*, Edited by Sussex Academic Press, 1997.
27. Patwant Singh: *The Guru and the Granth: A View Through World's Gurdwaras*, The Tribune, Februray, 21, 1993.
28. Pritam Singh Gill: *Heritage of Sikh Culture*, New Academic Publishing Company, Jullundur, 1975.
29. Prof. Harbans Singh (Edited): *The Encyclopaedia of Sikhism*, Punjabi University, Patiala, Vol. IV, 1998.
30. Satnam Kaur: *Three Basics of Sikh Religious Thought*, Pragati Publications, Delhi, 1997.
31. Shamsher Singh: *Sikh Philosophy and Spiritual Life*, 1999.
32. Sharad Chandra Verma: *Guru Nanak and the Logos of Divine Manifestation*, Delhi Gurdwara Prabhandhak Committee, 1967.
33. Sher Singh: *Philosophy of Sikhism*, Starling Publishers, New Delhi, 1966.
34. S.S. Kapoor: *The Sikh Religion and the Sikh People*, Hemkunt Press, New Delhi, 1992.

35. S.S. Kohli: *Travels of Guru Nanak*, Punjab University, Chandigrah, 1969.
36. Surjit Singh Gandhi: *Sikhs in the Eighteenth Century*, Singh Brothers, Amritsar, 1999.
37. Surjit Singh Gandhi: "*Nanak IX-Guru Tegh Bahadur*", in *History of the Sikhs And Their Religion*, Vol. I, Edited by Kirpal Singh and Kharak Singh, Shiromani Gurdwara Prabandhak Committee, Amritsar, 2004
38. Trilochan Singh: *Chapters on Historical Sikh Shrines in Delhi*, *Fundamental Beliefs of Sikh Religion and The Ten Masters*. Delhi Sikh Gurdwara Board, Sisganj, Delhi, 1972.
39. Vivek Ranjan Bhattacharya: *Secular Thoughts of the Sikh Gurus*, Gian Publishing House, Delhi, 1988.
40. Wazir Singh: *Philosophy of Sikh Religion*, ESS Publication, 1981.
41. William Irvine: *Later Mughals*, 2 Vols. London, 1922.

Acknowledgements

My endeavor to pursue an in-depth study of the Historical Gurdwaras of Delhi was initially perpetuated by a galaxy of Sikh scholars specially Dr. Jaspal Singh, Sdr. Kulmohan Singh and Dr. Gurdeep Singh Virdi. I express my deep gratitude to them all. I wish to record my earnest thanks for the help and valuable suggestions offered by Late Sdr. Surinder Singh Johar, Dr. Harbans Singh Chawla, Dr. Paramvir Singh, Dr. Harjinder Singh Dilgeer, Sdr. Kulwinder Singh and Shri Anoop Asthana. I would like to thank the Granthis and the Information Officers of the concerned Historical Gurdwaras who have extended unstinted help and co-operation in many different ways during my field investigations in Delhi. I have no words to express how deeply grateful I feel to every member of Niyogi Books for their help and co-operation at all times.

Index